# The
# Right
# Path

# The
# Right
# Path

**Choosing the right path in life and ministry**

## By Dr. Paul Chappell

**SWORD of the LORD PUBLISHERS**

Post Office Box 1099 • Murfreesboro, Tennessee 37133

# Dedication

In a day when many Christian leaders are abandoning the "old paths," I wish to express my gratitude to men of God who, by His grace, have not altered their God-given course. In particular, I dedicate this book to my dear friend Dr. R. B. Ouellette who encourages me and walks with me in the service of our Lord.

# Contents

# Acknowledgments

A special word of thanks to my wife, Terrie, and our four children, Danielle, Larry, Kristine, and Matthew, for their love and encouragement in the ministry.

I would also like to express my gratitude to Mrs. Lisa Stoner, Mrs. Julie Jenkins, and Miss Melanie Anderson for their help in typing this manuscript. Thanks for serving with a cheerful spirit!

I also appreciate the layout assistance of Mr. Craig Parker. I'm proud of you, Craig!

Cary Schmidt has served with me at Lancaster Baptist Church for over a decade, and I appreciate the input and creativity. Thanks for sharing the vision!

A special thanks to Dr. Shelton Smith, Guy King, and the entire team at the Sword of the Lord for their commitment to Christ and help in this project.

Finally, I praise our Lord Jesus for lovingly leading me in the paths of righteousness. My prayer is to walk in His steps.

# Introduction

Twenty years ago I was ordained into the gospel ministry. I will never forget that September night as a group of pastors and deacons gathered around me to pray that God would bless and use my life.

I am thankful that when the Lord called me to serve Him, I chose to follow.

The Christian life is a series of choices: choices to follow or not to follow—choices like walking by faith or walking by sight, walking in the Spirit or walking in the flesh.

Every Christian has the opportunity to say yes to the Lord every day. And when we do, He delights in walking with us and leading us in paths of righteousness and blessing.

The critical path to spiritual joy and a fulfilling life purpose is not found on a diagram or a chart but is clearly found in God's Word.

The psalmist described it this way:

> *"Thou wilt shew me the path of life: in thy presence is fulness of joy; at thy right hand there are pleasures for evermore."* —Psalm 16:11.

> *"Thy word is a lamp unto my feet, and a light unto my path."* —Psalm 119:105.

The best choices I have ever made have been choices made on the path of fellowship with God and in the light of His Word.

Besides endeavoring to follow the right path in my own life, it has been my joy for the past seventeen years to challenge a wonderful church family to follow Christ. While our church family has grown from that original group of a few dozen people to several thousand, we are still on the same path, making the same daily choice to follow Jesus.

Sometimes, however, we as Christians will grow weary and be tempted to stray from the safe and proven pathway of Scripture. It is my prayer that the lessons and truths contained in this book would be used of the Lord to help you and encourage you as follow in His steps.

As you journey through this book you will be encouraged to "stay the course" in your walk with God personally and in your ministry for the Lord as His servant.

May God bless you as you choose to follow "The Right Path."

# Setting the Course

This book is designed to help you set the right course for your personal and ministry life. Each chapter brings out critical principles that are worthy of review and application. At the end of each chapter you will find a section entitled "Setting the Course." Before you move on, take a moment to reflect upon the questions and to make decisions that the Lord might place upon your heart.

You might also consider using these questions in group or class settings for discussion or further follow-up.

May God bless you as you choose the right path and set the right course for your life!

## CHAPTER ONE

# The Right Heart

## Serving God With a Pure Heart

*"Blessed are the pure in heart: for they shall see God."*
Matthew 5:8

We live in a society that is constantly telling us that experiences and possessions will bring happiness to our lives. The travel agencies promote travel as the key to excitement. Car companies say it is in owning a certain model of car. Friends at work sometimes talk about things that they have accomplished or things that they possess. They tell us that these things have brought great joy to their lives. Yet as soon as that new car has a dent in it or the vacation is over and the bills come in, the joy starts to subside.

The mature Christian is one who really knows that experiences and possessions, apart from character in our hearts, are empty illusions. True joy comes from a heart relationship with the Lord Jesus Christ.

> *The mature Christian knows that experiences and possessions, apart from character, are empty illusions.*

During a trip with my wife to Los Angeles to make some hospital visits, I took a wrong turn. (I was not lost, of course.) While trying to figure out where we were, we began to reminisce about our early days of marriage.

Our first apartment was in Upland, California. It was just a one-bedroom apartment with a bed and a chair. That was it. We ate on the chair, talked on that chair, and spent a lot of time together on that one chair. It was a recliner that wouldn't close. We talked about how we had enjoyed our meals—macaroni and cheese several times a week. My wife had learned to make macaroni and cheese many different ways.

As we discussed that particular time in our lives, I asked, "Honey, could you truly be happy if we were to go there, right now today, and live in that apartment under those same circumstances?"

She said, "If we were right with God and had the love

of God, I most certainly could be happy there."

Now that is the sign of somebody truly content in her heart with the Lord. A truly grateful person realizes that the undeserved physical blessings of life do not bring happiness.

Oftentimes a newly married couple start to buy things they "need." In two to three years, they find themselves heavily in debt and in need of marriage counseling to find the missing joy in their life. Much of my life is spent counseling people who believe that a change of circumstances instead of a change of heart is what they need.

My parents were missionaries in Seoul, South Korea, during my teen years, and I can remember the first several months being very difficult for me. In the States, I had just started high school, had made the football team, and was looking forward to getting my driver's license when my parents announced that we would be moving to Korea.

Though the idea of moving to another country was somewhat exciting, it was also a very lonely feeling. During those first several months, I was especially unhappy. Looking back, I can see that my heart was rebellious toward the will of God. I was upset in being uprooted from my friends. At the time, I was certain that the reason I was so unhappy was the place where I lived. I was convinced that the problem was my surroundings, the language barrier—anything but me.

However, there came a point in my life when I heard a message preached, went to an altar to pray, and got some things right in my heart. To the glory of God, I can say that my life was changed and my joy renewed. I did not even have to move out of South Korea for that to happen. I just needed to get my heart right.

## The Definition of a Pure Heart

In Matthew 5:8 we read, "Blessed are the pure in heart..." When God uses the term "heart," it is not referencing the muscle that pumps blood through the body; instead, it means the whole inner self, the totality of the innermost being.

Proverbs 3:5, 6 states, "Trust in the LORD with all thine heart; and lean not unto thine own understanding. In all thy ways acknowledge him, and he shall direct thy paths." The Bible speaks of the heart as being the seat of our emotions. John 14:1 says, "Let not your heart be troubled: ye believe in God, believe also in me." The heart also impacts our intellect. "...Why reason ye these things in your hearts?" (Mark 2:8).

The heart is the place where our will resides and where our decisions are made. Daniel 1:8 states, "But Daniel purposed in his heart that he would not defile himself with the portion of the king's meat...." The heart affects the emotions, the intellect, and

> *The heart is where our will resides, where our decisions are made.*

the will. For instance, when somebody accepts Jesus as his Saviour, he is exercising his will from the heart.

The Bible says in Ephesians 3:17, "That Christ may dwell in your hearts by faith...." Christ indwells the innermost being of a believer, that person who puts his faith in Jesus Christ.

While I was talking with a couple about Christ and the Gospel, the wife began to ask questions about whether she would be accepted by God or by a church. I began to share with her the love of God.

It was not long before she prayed at her kitchen table and accepted Jesus Christ into her heart by faith according to the Word of God. It was a decision made from her heart.

So, what does the Bible mean when it states, "Blessed are the pure in heart..."? The word "pure" is not used much in our tainted society. The Word of God is perfect and pure. Scriptures tell us that God wants our hearts to become purified through His Word. Being pure means having no guile. A pure heart is a heart that is sincere and without hypocrisy. It is fixed on God and the Lord Jesus Christ, not double-minded.

Recently, an army officer accused a highly acclaimed naval officer of wearing medals on his uniform that were not rightfully his. The army colonel began an Internet campaign, speaking out against the admiral. A year later the news reported that the admiral committed suicide. The personal attack was so painful and devastating that he simply took his life as a way to escape the situation. It was later discovered that the colonel who made the accusation had also been wearing medals which were not rightfully his. What caused such a devastating event? The duplicity of the heart of someone acting like he was a purist, when in reality there was impurity in his own life.

Christians can be just as guilty for acting as if everything is right with God when it is not. The Bible says in Jeremiah 32:39, "And I will give them one heart...." God says that when you are right with Him, there will be a singleness of mind, and your heart will thirst for God.

When a Christian has this singleness of mind, he will ask himself, "What would Jesus do in this situation?" The psalmist said in Psalm 57:7, "My heart is fixed, O God, my heart is fixed...." His heart was firmly established in his relationship with God.

One of the greatest challenges of the Christian life is keeping one's heart established and fixed on God, while being tossed to and fro by the world. When someone's heart is fixed on God, then there is stability in the home, the church, and on the job. When the relationship is right "vertically" with our Saviour, then relationships "horizontally" will function accordingly.

A few years back I was on an airplane when the pilot came on and said, "Ladies and gentlemen, we are going to be delayed from takeoff this afternoon. We have a light here in the cockpit telling us that there may be some problems with the fuel system. We just want to take care of the problem."

I was thinking that it was good that they were taking care of the problem before leaving the ground. There were others on that plane that were already half drunk and complaining about not staying on schedule. I felt like asking them if they would rather stay on schedule and die, or get things right and stay alive.

It took about two hours before the pilot let us know that the problem had been fixed. The plane took off and landed safely with everything working fine. As I unloaded at the airport, I saw dozens of airplanes that all looked great from the outside, but some of them may also have had internal problems that would cause severe devastation if not fixed.

It is the same way in churches today. A person may look fine from the outside, but God sees each heart. How is your heart? Have you been acting with duplicity, or is your heart pure?

# The Development of a Pure Heart

The heart is deceitful. The Bible says in Jeremiah 17:9, "The heart is deceitful above all things, and desperately wicked: who can know it?"

Feelings or instincts cannot be trusted. Our heart, according to the Bible, can mislead us because we are fallen creatures tainted with a sin nature. Once someone accepts the Lord as Saviour, he becomes a new creature with a new spirit; however, there is still the old flesh—a deceitful, wicked nature that can hinder spiritual growth.

The Bible warns in James 1:26, "If any man among you seem to be religious, and bridleth not his tongue, but deceiveth his own heart, this man's religion is vain." We can shoot our heart with religious "novocaine," giving ourselves the sensation that everything is okay when it is not. I cannot be the spiritual judge of my own heart. I must put my heart on trial before God and ask for His convicting eyes to search and try me. Every Christian should have this heart attitude when attending church or reading the Word of God. The hearts of His people should remain open.

David wrote in Psalm 139:23, "Search me, O God, and know my heart: try me, and know my thoughts." On a regular basis, we should take time out of busy schedules to get alone with God and let Him examine our hearts.

A pure heart can be developed through honesty and transparency with God. It is so easy to have a lack of real vulnerability or transparency in our relationships. We make it our habit to act as though everything were right before God, but God is not deceived. He knows

*A pure heart can be developed through honesty with God.*

our hearts. He loves us and is merciful towards us. As a loving Father, He will show us and guide us into the realm of having a pure heart.

As God examines the heart, He will change the heart. Jeremiah 24:7 states, "And I will give them an heart to know me...." Once I have opened my heart to Him, I must have a willing attitude to change the things He shows me to change. After making these changes, I must ask the Lord to guard my heart from temptations that may affect the changes I have made.

When you are close to God, it is a very precious time. Yet that spiritual intimacy can quickly slip away with one wrong joke, one wrong movie, one wrong attitude, one family feud, or one sinful act. The intimacy with God that was once known fades, and the fellowship is lost.

It is critical that a Christian guard his heart. That is what the Bible means in Proverbs 4:23: "Keep thy heart with all diligence; for out of it are the issues of life." The word "keep" means to set up a gate around it, to watch your heart at all times. Sometimes throughout the daily routine of life, the heart can become very sinful in its thought process.

No one immediately becomes involved in the wicked sin of immorality. It starts in the heart. The heart of every sin problem is a problem of the heart. At the first wrong thought, a guard should go up. We need to tell Satan to get behind us for our heart is the Lord's.

Why do Christians struggle? Perhaps it is because many times we want to live for the Devil six days a week and live for God on Sunday. We need to guard our hearts seven days a week. Wrong attitudes can creep into the heart without the Christian's realizing it. Do not let sinful attitudes and thoughts keep you from loving God with all of your heart, soul, and mind.

Our society is changing so subtly and yet so rapidly that sometimes we become accustomed to wrong things. I am shocked that now prime-time television flaunts homosexuality and lesbianism. Christians who would have been shocked and outraged a few years ago have become apathetic and even interested in these sinful actions. That is the sign of a people who have let the guard down from their hearts.

In 1946, theaters were getting ready for the first run of

the movie *It's a Wonderful Life*. As the movie was being reviewed, there were some things that were censored from the movie before it could be shown around the country.

Critics said that the words *jerk, lousy, God, impotent,* and *garlic eater* were considered bad and could not be used. This took place just over fifty years ago. Think about our movie industry today. Children can hear and see the vilest words, actions, and scenes that you could ever imagine. Sadly enough, it does not even shock the average Christian. Why? Because the guard has been dropped from around our hearts.

Parents will set up guard posts for their children, but what about themselves? Do they think that bad movies will not affect their marriages or their thought processes? If it is wrong for the children, it is wrong for their parents also.

The Bible clearly states in Matthew 5:8, "Blessed are the pure in heart: for they shall see God." Do you really want to see God working in your life, in your family, and in your workplace? It begins with developing a pure heart.

## The Destination of a Pure Heart

To the spiritual man, there is nothing higher than

intimacy with God. There is no greater thrill. The treasure of a spiritual man or woman is closeness with God. The phrase "shall see God" does not refer to a literal viewing of God the Heavenly Father.

The Bible tells us in John 1:18, "No man hath seen God at any time; the only begotten Son, which is in the bosom of the Father, he hath declared him." First Timothy 6:16: "Who only hath immortality, dwelling in the light which no man can approach unto; whom no man hath seen, nor can see: to whom be honour and power everlasting. Amen." Even when Moses was in the presence of God, he saw merely the glory of God. The Bible referred to it as the "hind part," or the back.

What is the Bible referring to when it says we can see God? It simply means that we can experience intimacy with God personally. We can see God at work in numerous ways when we have a pure heart.

First, we can see Him in creation. Psalm 19:1 states, "The heavens declare the glory of God; and the firmament sheweth his handywork." When you see the Grand Canyon or the Sierra Nevada mountains, you are not seeing an accident of man, but rather the purposeful creation of God. Through His creation, you and I can see God every day.

We can also see God in the circumstances of our lives. Someone who is pure in heart sees everything as sacred. Paul wrote in Romans 8:28, "And we know that all things work together for good to them that love God, to them who are the called according to his purpose."

God's hand is moving and working in all the affairs of men, even in the tragedies. Life is a series of appointments with God. A pure-hearted Christian is not cynical. He does not blame God or question why, because he knows that God is working all things for His honor and glory. Someone who struggles with having a pure heart will often be cynical or discouraged. Nothing catches our God by surprise, and with Him there are no accidents.

God can also be seen in His Word. John 5:39 reads, "Search the scriptures; for in them ye think ye have eternal life: and they are they which testify of me." The Scriptures will testify of God when Christ is not physically present. We can know God through the Word of God. Many times Christians read other books, even good Christian books, more than the Bible. You will not see God apart from reading His Word, for the Word testifies of Him.

Is your heart pure before Him today? Have you allowed some things to creep into your life that need to be thrown out? Have you set up a guard around your heart? The highest joy of man comes from cultivating the deepest part of man—the heart. When the heart is pure, the vision is clear.

> *The highest joy of man comes from cultivating the deepest part of man—the heart.*

Sometimes the reason that our vision is not clear is that our heart is not pure. As long as you have a pure heart, you can expect to see God work in your life. When a heart becomes filled with sin, cynicism, or fleshly attributes, God cannot be seen nor His presence felt.

I challenge you to experience the highest joy known to man as you cultivate the deepest part of your life. Develop a right heart before God and then allow Him to lead you on the right path.

# Setting the Course

1. What is the world's perception of what brings joy and happiness? How does this viewpoint change for the Christian?

   _____

   _____

   _____

2. What is the key to maintaining a pure heart for the Lord?

   _____

   _____

   _____

3. What is the root cause of a Christian's straying from a close relationship with the Lord?

   _____

   _____

   _____

4. Because the heart is deceitful, the believer must be like David in Psalm 139:23 and do what?

   _____

   _____

   _____

5. For the believer that is sincere, what does God promise in Jeremiah 24:7?

_____

_____

_____

6. In Matthew 5:8, the phrase "shall see God" is used. To what is the Bible referring when it states this?

_____

_____

_____

7. Someone that is struggling with having a pure heart will often display what type of attitude?

_____

_____

_____

8. In Proverbs 3:5, 6, Mark 2:8, and Daniel 1:8, we see that the heart can affect three areas of our lives. What are these three things?

_____

_____

_____

9. Finish this quote: *The highest _____ of man comes from _____ the _____ part of man—the _____.*

## CHAPTER TWO

# The Right Conscience

## Maintaining a Conscience Void of Offense

*"And herein do I exercise myself, to have always a conscience void of offence toward God, and toward men."*
Acts 24:16

**Imagine** that you were on trial, standing before a prosecuting attorney because you had been telling people about Jesus Christ. You might be thinking, "That would only happen in a Muslim country," and you may be right. Yet this type of persecution has existed since the early days of Christianity.

In Acts 24, this very scene unfolds in the life of the Apostle Paul. The high priest Ananias, the Sadducees, and the Pharisees are outraged. These men bring in an attorney by the name of Tertullus, an eloquent orator, to plead their case against Paul before Felix, the governor of Caesarea. In Acts 24:5, one of the accusations brought against Paul says, "For we have found this man a pestilent fellow, and a mover of sedition among all the Jews throughout the world, and a ringleader of the sect of the Nazarenes."

Throughout the first several verses these religious leaders of Paul's day try to discredit his ministry. It is the same today. Many are highly suspicious of churches and people that are trying to do the work of God. People will question actions and motives and perhaps even bring unfounded accusations against a pastor or godly Christians.

## The Dynamic of Conscience

In the midst of the trial, Paul finally says something in his defense in verse 16: "And herein do I exercise myself, to have always a conscience void of offence toward God, and toward men."

*What life does to us depends on what life finds in us.*

Someone once stated that what life does to us depends on what life finds in us. Even though Paul was being falsely accused, he was able to say that he had lived his life in such a way that he had a good testimony—a clear conscience before God and man. This should be the desire of every Christian.

The conscience is the inner faculty that, with the Holy Spirit, approves when we do right and convicts when we do wrong. The conscience can be described as a window in the soul that allows light into a situation, a light that reveals motives and hidden agendas of the heart. Accordingly, a right heart and a right conscience will always accompany each other.

Friend, God wants you to have a good conscience. The Bible says in Acts 23:1, "And Paul, earnestly beholding the council, said, Men and brethren, I have lived in all good conscience before God until this day." First Timothy 1:19 states, "Holding faith, and a good conscience; which some having put away concerning faith have made shipwreck." Second Timothy 1:3 says, "I thank God, whom I serve from my forefathers with pure conscience, that without ceasing I have remembrance of thee in my prayers night and day."

We should all desire to do our best in the ministry where God has allowed us to serve. We must strive to have a clear conscience toward God and toward man in all matters of ministry. Paul was able to write back to his churches with a clear conscience that he had done his very best for them.

## The Good Conscience

A good conscience is developed by the grace of God. The Bible says in Titus 2:11,12, "For the grace of God that bringeth salvation hath appeared to all men, Teaching us that, denying ungodliness and worldly lusts, we should live soberly, righteously, and godly, in this present world."

If we will follow the leadership of the Holy Spirit and grow in the grace and knowledge of the Lord Jesus Christ, we will have a good conscience when it comes to life and ministry. The Bible says in II Corinthians 1:12, "For our rejoicing is this, the testimony of our conscience, that in simplicity and godly sincerity, not with fleshly wisdom, but by the grace of God, we have had our conversation in the world, and more abundantly to you-ward."

As he served Christ, Paul stated that he kept a good testimony toward his fellowman. Why could he say this? He could say it because of the Holy Spirit at work within, controlling, guiding, and directing his life moment by moment. Even so, in our lives, when the flesh becomes angry, the Spirit of God will cause us to have love, joy, and peace by His grace. His work within us helps us to make the right decisions during moments of pressure or temptation.

Because Paul was a man of godliness, he was a man of grace. You cannot overemphasize the inner working of God's grace in your relationship with Him. The result of living with God's grace in your life will not be loose living; it will be Christlike living.

## The Defiled Conscience

Titus 1:15 says, "Unto the pure all things are pure: but unto them that are defiled and unbelieving is nothing pure; but even their mind and conscience is defiled."

It is amazing how a certain word can be said within a group of people that is not meant in a bad context, but someone will begin to laugh or joke about that particular word. Why? His conscience is defiled. Rather than having a good conscience, a pure conscience that is motivated by grace, he has started thinking in a fleshly pattern. With these thought patterns, our conscience becomes defiled.

In Titus 1:16 it says, "They profess that they know God; but in works they deny him, being abominable, and disobedient, and unto every good work reprobate."

The man with a defiled conscience is a man whose heart is not receiving the light of truth as clearly as he once did. He cannot sense the convicting presence of

27

God within. Yet a man who has a clear conscience with God regularly experiences the conviction of the Holy Spirit within his heart. Immediately he knows that he is not living the way that God would have him to live.

A defiled conscience prevents conviction from being felt. When defilement has entered the heart, it is as though a cloak has been placed over the convicting light of the Holy Spirit. The light may be shining, but it cannot be seen. The light cannot get through when someone's conscience has been defiled by sin. Over time, unconfessed sin in our hearts creates a defiled conscience, which creates a confused life. When the guide of a pure conscience has been defiled, we begin to walk in darkness.

*Unconfessed sin creates a defiled conscience.*

## The Evil Conscience

The Bible says in Hebrews 10:22, "Let us draw near with a true heart in full assurance of faith, having our hearts sprinkled from an evil conscience, and our bodies washed with pure water."

The evil conscience is a conscience that is constantly thinking evil thoughts. This happens over time to one with a defiled conscience.

First Thessalonians 5:19 says, "Quench not the Spirit." The Bible also says in Ephesians 4:30, "And grieve not the holy Spirit of God, whereby ye are sealed unto the day of redemption." The Christian heart can become numb to the conviction of the Holy Spirit.

There is a teaching today that seems to minimize the conscience in the heart of a Christian. This teaching denies any teaching about holy or right living, claiming that such teachings create false guilt in the heart of the Christian. Yet there is a vast difference between *guilt* and *Holy Spirit conviction*. When the Holy Spirit convicts us of sin, the result should not be guilt; it should be confession and repentance!

My friend, before we blame the Bible or the church for "false guilt," we had better make sure that our heart is right with God. Sensing conviction in your conscience is a privilege that you do not want to lose. If you develop the habit of ignoring the Holy Spirit's conviction, eventually you will stop feeling it!

Feeling conviction simply means that you can still sense God working within your heart, and the solution for an evil conscience is heartfelt repentance before God.

## The Seared Conscience

First Timothy 4:1,2 says, "Now the Spirit speaketh expressly, that in the latter times some shall depart from the faith, giving heed to seducing spirits, and doctrines of devils; Speaking lies in hypocrisy; having their conscience seared with a hot iron."

These verses present a tragic illustration. Have you ever burned yourself? If you have, then you know that after a time, burned skin becomes dead. There is no feeling or sensitivity in that spot. This is what it means to have a seared conscience. A person with a seared conscience will hear preaching but will feel no effects, or he may be one who is around Christians and has no sensitivity to God at work within his heart.

A seared conscience is so limited in its ability to feel the conviction of God that it becomes open to all sorts of deception and false beliefs. The Bible says in I Timothy 4:1, "Now the Spirit speaketh expressly, that in the latter times some shall depart from the faith, **giving heed to seducing spirits, and doctrines of devils.**"

As the Apostle Paul stood before the religious elite of his day, he could say he had served God with a clear conscience, void of offense toward God and man. This should be the goal of every Christian! We should serve the Lord with a good conscience, not living with an evil conscience nor with a defiled conscience nor with a seared conscience. We should be able to live every day with peace in our hearts that our conscience is clear before God and man.

# The Development of Conscience

How can we develop a conscience that is clear and that is exercised unto godliness? Some would say that it does not matter, because we are under grace. Their reasoning is that you can do whatever you want because of God's grace! Yet this kind of thinking will lead to a life that is not pleasing to our Saviour. It ought to be our heart's desire to please Him who has called us, and we must give ourselves to developing a conscience that is void of offense.

### Exercise Requires a Goal

Paul says in Acts 24:16, "And herein do I exercise myself, to have always a conscience void of offence toward God, and toward men." He says that having a conscience void of offense is something at which he had to work. Notice in the verse that he uses the word "exercise." Exercise requires a goal.

Paul gave us his goal in I Corinthians 9:25–27: "And every man that striveth for the mastery is temperate in all things. Now they do it to obtain a corruptible crown; but we an incorruptible. I therefore so run, not as uncertainly; so fight I, not as one that beateth the air: But I keep under my body, and bring it into subjection: lest that by any means, when I have preached to others, I myself should be a castaway."

Paul's goal was not for an earthly prize, but for a heavenly one. His goal was to please the Lord Jesus Christ. First Thessalonians 4:1 says, "Furthermore then we beseech you, brethren, and exhort you by the Lord Jesus, that as ye have received of us how ye ought to walk and to please God, so ye would abound more and more."

Even as the Olympic athletes exercise so that they can run a race within a certain time or lift a certain weight, Paul exercised himself to please God. What a tremendous goal for every Christian to strive to obtain!

In II Timothy 2:4, Paul said, "No man that warreth entangleth himself with the affairs of this life; that he may please him who hath chosen him to be a soldier."

As Christians, we are given biblical principles of separation in our lives so we do not become entangled in the affairs of this life to the point that we are no longer void of offense toward God and toward man. We are commanded to walk circumspectly so that our service to God before men will be void of offense.

Being involved in the ministry of Jesus Christ is a holy calling. It is a precious privilege, and we must own that privilege with a clear conscience. When I say or do something that I should not, I must be the first one to make that right before God and before men. Our heart's desire should be to live blamelessly, so we do not harm the work of Christ in the lives of others.

The goal of a clear conscience is not simply to conform to an outward list of rules. A list of rules by itself does not please Jesus Christ, but holy living from the heart does please Him. Following the life of Christ will mean that we will need to

*Our heart's desire should be to live blamelessly.*

choose to have some rules or guidelines for our behavior. As His Word gives us principles by which to live, we have the liberty to create guidelines to help us follow His Word. Our finished goal should always be to please Christ.

## Exercise Requires Discipline

In I Corinthians 9:27, Paul says it this way: "But I keep

under my body, and bring it into subjection: lest that by any means, when I have preached to others, I myself should be a castaway."

Paul was willing to buffet his body. He was willing to sacrifice things that were not necessarily evil but things that would hinder his work for Christ. There are some things as Christian leaders that we must be willing to lay aside to be more effective for Christ. These are things that might be weights in my own life or stumbling blocks in someone else's life.

This philosophy is not popular today among Christians. Many Christians want to be involved in ministry while still living like the unsaved world. God has commanded us, as spiritual leaders, to be transformed by Jesus Christ. "And be not conformed to this world: but be ye transformed by the renewing of your mind, that ye may prove what is that good, and acceptable, and perfect, will of God" (Romans 12:2).

If you are serious about having a clear conscience before God and before men, then be willing to live a life of discipline, laying aside things that could hinder you or harm others. You need to be willing to set aside your rights and liberties so that you can be the right influence on those who are following you.

# The Display of a Right Conscience

"And herein do I exercise myself, to have always a conscience void of offence toward God, and toward men" (Acts 24:16). Paul says that his life was a life lived for Christ that was void of offense. He had not brought reproach to the name of Jesus Christ.

## Void of Offense Toward God

No matter the money you make, the traffic you face, or the events of your day—the greatest joy of life is to put your head on the pillow at night and know that you have done your best for Jesus Christ. There is a great reward in just knowing that you have given your best for the Lord.

Paul makes it clear that this was his habit of life every day. He chose moment by moment to live in such a way that his heart was clear before the Lord. First Samuel 16:7 says, "But the LORD said unto Samuel, Look not on his countenance, or on the height of his stature; because I have refused him: for the LORD seeth not as man seeth; for man looketh on the outward appearance, but the LORD looketh on the heart."

Why did Paul say that his goal was to please God? Why did he say that he was void of offense toward man and toward God? I believe Paul recognized that it is God that tries our hearts.

As a Christian, your first priority ought to be that everything is right between you and God. You might sing in the choir or preach the Word of God and look great outwardly. You might have a new Bible, dress modestly, and act just right; yet if there is bitterness, lust, or anger in your heart, God sees that. Our first priority should be to live void of offense toward God.

> *There is a great reward in knowing that you have given your best for the Lord.*

God sees the heart. Personal standards are not the goal; leadership requirements are not the goal; Jesus is the goal. Honoring and glorifying Jesus Christ should be the goal of every Christian.

## Void of Offense Toward Men

Paul said that he was void of offense toward God and man. What a great life principle! What a great way to go to bed every night, knowing that you are right in your heart before God and before men!

The key to having a life void of offense toward men is

to live a godly lifestyle outwardly. In II Corinthians 4:2 Paul says, "But have renounced the hidden things of dishonesty, not walking in craftiness, nor handling the word of God deceitfully; but by manifestation of the truth commending ourselves to every man's conscience in the sight of God."

Paul said that he handled the Word of God in his life without deceit. His life was pure before God and man because he walked honestly. Every Christian does things that he regrets and has failures that he would like to undo. As spiritual leaders, we must desire to commend ourselves to every man's conscience in the sight of God. We must desire to live lives that will point others to Jesus Christ.

Paul was not concerned with his "rights" or "liberties" as a Christian leader. He was concerned with living in a way that pleased Jesus Christ and edified others. Notice in I Corinthians 8:9, Paul says to the church at Corinth, "But take heed lest by

*We must desire to live lives that will point others to Jesus Christ.*

any means this liberty of yours become a stumbling-block to them that are weak." A spiritual leader must think in this way.

We often have new Christians over to our home for fellowship and discipleship. Many of them have recently struggled with things like alcohol or other sinful patterns. As a Christian, I could say that it is okay for me to have a little wine. Yet, in addition to my biblical conviction against alcohol, it would be unwise for me to have liquor in my home to be used as a stumbling block for a younger believer. As a leader, I must avoid abusing my liberty in Christ so that others do not stumble because of me. This is the way spiritual leaders think and live.

"For if any man see thee which hast knowledge sit at meat in the idol's temple, shall not the conscience of him which is weak be emboldened to eat those things which are offered to idols; And through thy knowledge shall the weak brother perish, for whom Christ died?" (I Corinthians 8:10,11).

Paul is saying that just because a person is saved he should not use the liberty that comes with salvation to be a stumbling block to an unsaved person who could be watching.

"But when ye sin so against the brethren, and wound their weak conscience, ye sin against Christ. Wherefore, if meat make my brother to offend, I will eat no flesh while the world standeth, lest I make my brother to offend" (I Corinthians 8:12,13).

The idea is not to force the liberty issue to the point that a new believer or an unbeliever would stumble at our actions. The Apostle Paul is telling us that the display of righteousness is something that is important toward God but also important toward man. We display godly living before man by living a separated life.

We can also display godliness toward mankind through our witness and soulwinning. Paul wanted to speak the truth in the way that others could hear and be saved.

"But have renounced the hidden things of dishonesty, not walking in craftiness, nor handling the word of God deceitfully; but by manifestation of the truth commending ourselves to every man's conscience in the sight of God" (II Corinthians 4:2).

Once again, conscience is the faculty of mind which distinguishes between right and wrong. So the implication here is that the right kind of preaching (the manifestation of truth) combined with the right manner of life (not walking in craftiness) will be used by God to affirm in the conscience of unsaved people that they need to be saved. Paul wanted his manifestation of the truth and of a godly walk to convey to those to whom he was writing that he was saying what was right and real. This is why a clear conscience in a spiritual leader is so important. Our message and manner of living must be consistent so that others can follow our words and lifestyle.

With this kind of spiritual commitment, even personal standards of separation become tools to bring others to the Lord Jesus Christ. It is not about conforming to a list for the sake of appearance. It is about living blamelessly before a lost world so that they can see the Saviour. It is our goal that our living would never hinder our opportunity to witness for Christ.

> *Our message and manner of living must be consistent.*

When I was about twenty years of age, I worked for the Caterpillar Tractor Company. One of my jobs was to drive parts for the tractors down to Orange County. I would take the parts in, and tractor operators from all over that part of Orange County would come pick up their parts. When I made the trip, I would spend the rest of my workday there until it was time to lock up and return home.

On one occasion I had already delivered the parts, cleaned up the store, swept the floor, and tidied up. I was waiting for the clock to hit five so I could head back up to Los Angeles. As I was waiting, a man came into the store and startled me. He was one of the big shots from the headquarters of the company. He had a company car and a company phone, which was pretty big stuff back then. His name was Mr. Mossbarger. As soon as I saw him, I stood to attention and asked if he needed anything.

Ironically, he just wanted to sit down and relax. After a few moments, we started talking. We talked about Caterpillar tractors and John Deere tractors. We talked about construction and all types of other things. As we talked, it got to be a little bit late, but toward the last few minutes of the conversation I sensed in my heart that the Lord wanted me to tell this man about Jesus Christ. I felt a compulsion of the Lord to share the Gospel with him. Since I was a young college student, talking with a big executive about salvation made me embarrassed about witnessing.

I let the flesh take over instead of listening to the Holy Spirit, and I chose not to witness to Mr. Mossbarger. A few moments later he left. I locked up the store, got into my truck, and drove back to the city of industry.

Several days later, I was sorting the mail in our office when I noticed a company memo on top of all the mail. It simply said, "We regret to inform you that last evening Mr. Ray Mossbarger died in his home from complications due to the cancer treatments that he had been undergoing."

I remember reading that. For the first time in my life, someone that I had known personally died suddenly. I was shocked. Although I was a Bible college student preparing for ministry, I had missed a precious opportunity. I had no idea that this man had been struggling with cancer or undergoing treatments. I remember the feeling that came over me, and to this day I believe that my conscience is not void of offense toward that man. Perhaps you can think of a circumstance or situation in which your conscience was not void of offense.

In that instance I had failed, but I know that God used that in my life to help me to obey the Holy Spirit in future witnessing opportunities. God has used that failure to impress upon me the importance of living with a conscience void of offense toward God and toward man.

Recently, a group of students from West Coast Baptist College were ministering in the Philippines. At the end of a week of preaching, singing, and ministering, they arrived at a hotel for the final night of their stay. The hotel manager approached our vice president, Dr. Mark Rasmussen, and asked if they were Christians. After Dr. Rasmussen told him that they were Christians, the man asked what the difference was between a Catholic and a Christian. Dr. Rasmussen was then able to explain that salvation is a free gift, paid for by the blood of Jesus, not earned by a church's system of achievement. It was not long before the man prayed to receive Christ as Saviour.

According to the "Christian" culture we see in today's world, I wonder if people would even question whether some are Christians. Living a distinct and separated life unto Christ is important!

I am not referring to perfectionism. I am not referring to legalism. I am not referring to creating a system of mandating holiness. I am simply referring to growing as a Christian, growing in grace, growing in the life of Christ to the point that you can say that your conscience is clear toward God and toward man.

May God help us to recognize the dynamic of a right conscience. There is such a thing as a good conscience. May God help us to see the development of godliness. If we are going to be godly people, then we must have goals and the discipline to reach those goals spiritually. May we have a display of righteousness that God sees in our hearts and that people around us will see in our lives.

"But sanctify the Lord God in your hearts: and be ready always to give an answer to every man that asketh you a reason of the hope that is in you with meekness and fear: Having a good conscience; that, whereas they speak evil of you, as of evildoers, they may be ashamed that falsely accuse your good conversation in Christ" (I Peter 3:15,16).

# Setting the Course

1.  When the Apostle Paul stood before the court in Acts 24, what one thing was he able to say to them that lent credibility to his testimony?

    _____

    _____

    _____

2.  Define *conscience*.

    _____

    _____

    _____

3.  Write out a Scripture that tells the believer how to develop a good conscience.

    _____

    _____

    _____

4.  What causes the Christian not to feel the conviction of the Holy Spirit at times?

    _____

    _____

    _____

5. When the conscience is not cleared, but rather stays defiled, it is not long before the conscience becomes what?

_____

_____

_____

6. What two passages of Scripture deal with the importance of not hindering the Holy Spirit's work of conviction?

_____

_____

_____

7. A Christian with a seared conscience opens himself up to what potential danger?

_____

_____

_____

8. A clear conscience does not come without effort. In

fact, Paul uses what particular word in Acts 24:16 to describe the effort it does take?

_____

_____

_____

9.  In order for us as Christians not to become entangled in the affairs of this life, boundaries need to be set up. What are these boundaries for the Christian?

_____

_____

_____

10. What philosophy has become popular in some religious circles today that violates I Corinthians 9:27, Romans 12:1,2, and I Corinthians 8:9?

_____

_____

_____

11. As a Christian, what should be your first priority in your Christian walk?

_____

_____

_____

## CHAPTER THREE
# The Right Purpose
### Reviving the Stones of Purpose
### in Ministry

*"The words of Nehemiah the son of Hachaliah. And it came to pass in the month Chisleu, in the twentieth year, as I was in Shushan the palace, That Hanani, one of my brethren, came, he and certain men of Judah; and I asked them concerning the Jews that had escaped, which were left of the captivity, and concerning Jerusalem. And they said unto me, The remnant that are left of the captivity there in the province are in great affliction and reproach: the wall of Jerusalem also is broken down, and the gates thereof are burned with fire. And it came to pass, when I heard these words, that I sat down and wept, and mourned certain days, and fasted, and prayed before the God of heaven."*
Nehemiah 1:1–4

One of the most devastating days in Jewish history took place around 586 B.C. when the Babylonian captivity began. When the Babylonians invaded Jerusalem, the Bible records that the temple was burned and the walls destroyed. Heartache filled the land.

About a hundred years later, a faithful remnant came back to rebuild the temple, and yet thousands of Jews remained outside of the land in captivity. One such man was Nehemiah. Though he was several hundred miles away, as soon as he heard the city was in peril, he prayerfully began to ask God to use him to make a difference for his people.

The Bible records that as Nehemiah began planning to rebuild the wall, opposition mounted and certain people began to fight against him.

I think about our stand on the Word of God as Bible-believing Christians. I believe that God desires to use the truth of His Word as a wall of protection in this land. Every Christian who would take a strong stand on the Word of God is a part of God's plan of spiritual protection for our great nation. The church is the pillar and ground of truth, and God has used His local churches in the past to be that spiritual wall.

Most of us can recall times when the wall of fundamental Christianity was much stronger. Some can recall times when it appeared that the gates were sturdy, the stones were set, and the hearts of our people were truly seeking after God. Souls were being saved and cities were being transformed.

Tragically, today our world stands in peril. Cities like New York, Los Angeles, and Atlanta stand in desperate need of revival. Yet in this needy hour, we see a weakening of convictions, a weakening of the wall of truth, a weakening and lessening of spiritual fervor. We can almost hear the enemies of the old-time religion as they stand around us and observe fundamental, Bible-believing Christians and somewhat scornfully ask the question, "Will they revive the stones out of the heaps of the rubbish?"

There are church growth experts who would say that

this idea of the old-time religion is something of the past that will never be effective again in our society. They say our ways and our messages are no longer useful. They say it is just a bunch of rubbish that can no longer be blessed of God in this day.

Now, we all would have to admit that within our lives there exist wood, hay, and stubble. In our churches, there is a good amount of rubbish—wood, hay, and stubble. Yet there are still some stones in the pile of rubbish; and if revived, God could use them again to make a great and mighty difference in this day.

Nehemiah revived three stones from the rubble of Jerusalem. Three right attributes or characteristics must be revived in our lives if we are going to rebuild this wall and reclaim what God has intended for our churches and for our world. If once again we are going to provide the spiritual leadership and influence that God intends for us to provide, these stones must be brought out of the rubbish heap.

# Reviving the Stone of Prayer

Upon hearing the tragic news of how the city lay in waste, the Bible says in verse 4 that Nehemiah "sat down and wept, and mourned certain days, and fasted, and prayed before the God of heaven." Take note that the first act of Nehemiah was the act of prayer.

*What we need is the anointing and power of God on our lives.*

Anything done in our own strength is going to fail miserably or succeed even more miserably. We do not need a better program. What we need is the anointing and power of God on our lives. Just as Nehemiah recognized that he could do nothing without God, we should realize that we can do nothing without the power and strength of Jesus Christ.

We see here the stone of prayer. It began with a man who was truly burdened for his city and whose heart was heavy. As a spiritual leader, Nehemiah saw the need and wept and mourned. The Bible teaches that he agonized and began to fast, denying himself and bringing prayer to its fullest development.

**The Prayer of a Burdened Heart**

Nehemiah wanted to see Jerusalem protected once again. He desired to see God's hand working in and through his life. He began to pray the prayer of an exercised soul. I am afraid that many times we get too busy to feel the burden that God wants us to feel. Most

Christians are more interested in what time the service is over, so they can get to the smorgasbord or get home to watch the ball game, than they are in hearing the Word of God.

I heard of a dad who was driving to McDonald's with his son when they saw a terrible car accident. The dad mentioned to the son that they should pray about the accident and the people involved. The little boy folded his hands, bowed his head and said, "Dear God, don't let these cars block our way to McDonald's."

In much the same way, America is lying in waste. Our churches are filled with materialism and self-centeredness. Our main concerns are those of our own fleshly lusts. They revolve around self rather than the will of God. Many preachers have lost the prayerful burden for revival.

> "We are too busy to pray, and so we are too busy to have power."

R. A. Torrey once said, "We are too busy to pray, and so we are too busy to have power. We have a great deal of activity but have accomplished very little. We have many services, but few conversions; much machinery, but very few results." Where are the men of God who will say, "I am tired of just having a service. I am tired of just singing songs and saying some words. God, we need to see revival in this land"?

## A Prayer That Burned With Compassion

Nehemiah's prayer burned with compassion. In Nehemiah 1:6 the Bible says, "Let thine ear now be attentive, and thine eyes open, that thou mayest hear the prayer of thy servant, which I pray before thee now, day and night, for the children of Israel thy servants, and confess the sins of the children of Israel, which we have sinned against thee: both I and my father's house have sinned."

In this particular verse, we see the compassion of Nehemiah's heart for those who were in peril in Jerusalem. His concern was for others. His care was like that of the Lord Jesus Christ who looked upon the fields and saw them white unto harvest and had great compassion on lost souls. Nehemiah's heart burned with compassion for those in Jerusalem.

There are people in your city who are looking for somebody to care for them. They are looking for someone to have compassion on them. I read recently that the world's population now stands at roughly six billion. In the next half century the total will increase by about three billion more. Ninety-five percent of that growth will occur in developing countries. Cities in the Middle East, Africa, and Latin America will teem with lost souls who need Jesus Christ.

While the humanist would tell us to offer social, technological, and medical help to these countries, we have a calling from God to introduce them to Jesus Christ. Oh, that God would revive true, Christlike compassion in our hearts! While we thank God for those who would feed a hungry child, may we have compassion on those who will spend all of eternity without Christ.

> *Oh, that God would revive true, Christlike compassion in our hearts!*

## A Prayer of Confession

Nehemiah's prayer was also one that was built on confession. In the latter portion of Nehemiah 1:6 the Bible says, "...and confess the sins of the children of Israel, which we have sinned against thee: both I and my father's house have sinned." Notice the personal reference, "both I and my father's house." Revival will not come to America until confession and repentance begin in the hearts of Christians.

57

Nehemiah came to a place where he said, "God, if there is something in my heart that needs to be dealt with, I want to confess it. I want to make it right." He was not just confessing the sins of the people.

In Proverbs 28:13 the Bible says, "He that covereth his sins shall not prosper: but whoso confesseth and forsaketh them shall have mercy." Proverbs 21:2 says, "Every way of a man is right in his own eyes: but the LORD pondereth the hearts." May we as Christians be willing to come to God with a willingness to confess our sin before Him. May we have a resistance toward the flesh, toward pride, and toward divisiveness in our churches. We should ask God to help us not have anything in our lives that might hinder revival.

## A Prayer Based on God's Word

Nehemiah's prayer was based on the Word of God. In Nehemiah 1:8,9, the Bible says, "Remember, I beseech thee, the word that thou commandedst thy servant Moses, saying, If ye transgress, I will scatter you abroad among the nations: But if ye turn unto me, and keep my commandments, and do them; though there were of you cast out unto the uttermost part of the heaven, yet will I gather them from thence, and will bring them unto the place that I have chosen to set my name there."

I love to read the Old Testament prophets when they quote God's own words back to Him while praying. Here we see Nehemiah is praying based upon the Word of God.

The ministry is not *our* idea but *God's*. The chief end of prayer is that God would be glorified in the answer. When we pray for souls, for revival, and in the way the Word of God has dictated, we can expect results. If we are faithful to pray according to the Book, God's Word will not return void, even in our prayer lives.

> *The chief end of prayer is that God would be glorified in the answer.*

If we want to see walls rebuilt and God's blessing on our churches again, we must revive the stone of prayer.

When people have asked what we are doing at Lancaster Baptist Church to make it grow, we gladly share some of the things God is blessing. Honestly, there is no secret formula. It is the basic things that God blesses.

One of the basic things in which our church has seen God bless is the Saturday night prayer meetings. Many of the men of the church will gather across our auditorium every Saturday night to pray that God will work in hearts and lives on Sunday morning. He is blessing the prayers of the ushers on Sunday mornings at 7:30 as they pray at each pew for those that will sit there that may not be saved. There is no replacement for a prayer life that causes us to come boldly to the throne of grace.

# Reviving the Stone of Purpose

Nehemiah also revived the stone of purpose. Prayer will always set a godly direction and purpose in life. Vision that comes from prayer will become a great motivator in our lives. The greater the prayer life, the clearer the vision will be; and the clearer the vision, the stronger the motivation will be.

Scripture is clear when it says in Matthew 5:8, "Blessed are the pure in heart: for they shall see God." We begin in prayer, and God helps our hearts to be made right with Him. We can stand to our feet, not giving our best idea or thought, but giving the very heart of God in the matter. We can say this is the purpose that God has given to us.

Notice the purpose of Nehemiah: "When Sanballat the Horonite, and Tobiah the servant, the Ammonite, heard of it, it grieved them exceedingly that there was come a man to seek the welfare of the children of Israel" (2:10). Sanballat and Tobiah knew the purpose of

Nehemiah's life was to seek the welfare of the children of Israel. What a blessing it would be if every city in America would have such a man! Nehemiah was that kind of a man.

We live in a troubled country. We do not test shampoo on animals, but we harvest human body parts from our unborn children. In the last fifteen years, the number of women in prison has increased by four hundred percent. Seventy-five percent of all women in prison are mothers, and their children are being reared without them.

But Nehemiah did not go to Jerusalem to pass out birth control or food stamps. Nehemiah's concern was the spiritual welfare of these people, that they might be protected to worship and that God would reign in their midst once again. His purpose was clear and it was God given!

## A Purpose of Personal Involvement

Nehemiah's purpose required personal involvement. Notice what the Bible says in chapter 2, verse 17: "Then said I unto them, Ye see the distress that we are in, how Jerusalem lieth waste, and the gates thereof are burned with fire: come, and let us build up the wall of Jerusalem, that we be no more a reproach."

When we take the stone of prayer into our hands and

into our hearts, God begins to give us a biblical purpose for the ministry. This purpose must be something we believe in so strongly that we will go alone with God if that is what it takes. If you are the only one out winning souls, you will still go. Nehemiah's purpose caused him to become personally involved.

There is no replacement for your presence in serving God. We need people like the deacons in Acts 6, who were among the people, with the people, serving along with them.

For the past several years, our church has been blessed with an average weekly attendance of between 400 and 600 on soulwinning visitation. Every week hundreds of people are going out and knocking on doors, visiting class members, and leading people to Christ. These soulwinners go for a number of reasons—the Word of God commands them, the love of Christ is constraining them, and the grace of God is moving them. Part of the equation is the fact that they see a pastoral staff among them going out as well!

My wife and I had a wonderful time knocking on doors recently. It keeps the ministry fresh for us week after week. Yes, we are busy with administration; but we are going to keep the main thing, the main thing, and the main thing is soulwinning. The Son of Man has come to seek and to save that which is lost. Just as Nehemiah's purpose required personal involvement, so our purpose requires our personal involvement!

Do not let go of this matter of soulwinning. Somehow this matter of becoming personally involved is slipping away. If there would be a revival of soulwinning amongst Christians, there would be a great moving in our nation once again with people coming to Christ.

> *If there would be a revival of soulwinning, there would be a great moving with people coming to Christ.*

## A Purpose Shared by the People

Nehemiah's purpose was also shared by the people. Nehemiah 2:17,18 says, "Then said I unto them, Ye see the distress that we are in, how Jerusalem lieth waste, and the gates thereof are burned with fire: come, and let us build up the wall of Jerusalem, that we be no more a reproach. Then I told them of the hand of my God which was good upon me; as also the king's words that he had spoken unto me. And they said, Let us rise up and build. So they strengthened their hands for this good work."

As Nehemiah himself exemplified positive leadership, others began to share in that vision. Seeing God's people getting together to do what God has called them to do is a wonderful thing.

We praise God for what He is doing at Lancaster Baptist Church. I have often said, "We give God the glory and our people the credit." We have found that teamwork truly does make the dream work.

I heard of a preacher who said during a sermon to his congregation, "Folks, I believe God wants this church to walk. I believe God wants this church to start walking."

*Teamwork makes the dream work.*

A fellow in the front row said, "Let it walk, Lord; let it walk."

As the message continued, the preacher said, "I believe God wants this church to start running. I really do—I really believe God wants the church to run."

The man in front said, "Yes, let it run, Lord."

After a while, the preacher said, "I believe God wants this church to fly. I really believe God wants the church to just take off and fly."

The church member once again said, "Mmm, Lord, let it fly."

As the preacher continued preaching he said, "If we are going to fly, it is going to take some money to fly."

The man in front said, "Let it walk, Lord; let it walk."

I am glad God has enabled me to pastor a people who strengthen their hands for the work through their giving, serving, and soulwinning. In I Samuel 14:7 Jonathan's armor-bearer said to Jonathan, "Do all that is in thine heart: turn thee; behold, I am with thee according to thy heart." When God's purpose is shared, God is glorified in the church!

In Nehemiah 2:20 the Bible says, "Then answered I them, and said unto them, The God of heaven, he will prosper us; therefore we his servants will arise and build: but ye have no portion, nor right, nor memorial, in Jerusalem."

When God's man gets a hold on God's purpose and God's people come around that godly purpose, God will be glorified once again in a community. We will look at what God is doing in our churches and say, as the psalmist, "This is the LORD's doing; it is marvellous in our eyes." Yes, the stone of prayer must be revived out of the rubbish.

# Reviving the Stone of Persistence

The third stone that Nehemiah revived was the stone of persistence. It is amazing to me that the wall was built in fifty-two days. In these modern times, you cannot get a permit in fifty-two days. It just does not happen that way in today's society! Yet these people under the leadership of Nehemiah put their hand to the work. They began to follow persistently the purpose God had given them.

## Persistence Through Ridicule

Notice that Nehemiah was persistent even when he was ridiculed. The Bible says in Nehemiah 2:19, "But when Sanballat the Horonite, and Tobiah the servant, the Ammonite, and Geshem the Arabian, heard it, they laughed us to scorn, and despised us, and said, What is this thing that ye do? will ye rebel against the king?"

Sanballat and Tobiah were men of wicked intent. They were anti-God and the enemies of God and His people.

They literally despised the work of God.

Every noble work of faith will at first seem impossible and will be criticized, tried, and tested. In the Scriptures, you will see that Satan fights against the work of God time and again. We must never allow these trials to divert our focus from our God-given purposes. We must never lose sight of the cross of Jesus Christ and His calling upon our lives.

Recently, I heard of a salesman who called a pastor's home. A little girl answered the phone. He said, "Hello, may I speak to your father, please."

> *Every noble work of faith will at first seem impossible and will be criticized, tried, and tested.*

She said, "Daddy can't come to the phone right now, because he is praying. A much larger church than ours has called him and asked him to come be the pastor. He is praying about it right now."

He said, "Well, may I talk to your mother then?"

The little girl said, "Oh, she can't come to the phone right now—she is packing."

Sometimes we are like that. We want to run at the first

sign of trouble or at the first opportunity that seems a little brighter. I believe with all of my heart, the best way to deal with criticism is to accomplish the task that God has given to you. Oftentimes the door of opportunity swings on the hinges of opposition. Difficult days will come. In II Corinthians 4:1 Paul said, "Therefore seeing we have this ministry, as we have received mercy, we faint not." He was saying, We are not going to stop; we are going to continue on, even in the day of adversity.

Nehemiah was persistent through ridicule. When ridicule and heartache come to your ministry or your life, I challenge you to get a pocketful of tracts and a heartful of love and go out and tell somebody else about Jesus Christ. Stay the course and continue fulfilling your purpose for the Lord Jesus Christ.

## Persistence Through Discouragement

Nehemiah was persistent when he was discouraged. Notice in Nehemiah 4:10: "And Judah said, The strength of the bearers of burdens is decayed, and there is much rubbish; so that we are not able to build the wall." There are problems within his own people. They tend not to focus on the potential of the wall but to focus on the rubbish.

Sometimes you will get around people who want to

focus on the rubbish and the problems instead of the stones. They have lost purpose and become bitter. The Bible says, "Make no friendship with an angry man." God has called us to speak the truth in love and to maintain a heart of love for our brothers in Christ.

In this passage, the people of Judah began to focus on the problems by listening to the adversary in verse 11: "And our adversaries said, They shall not know, neither see, till we come in the midst among them, and slay them, and cause the work to cease." At this point there was great discouragement building among the people.

Yet in verse 14, Nehemiah says, "And I looked, and rose up, and said unto the nobles, and to the rulers, and to the rest of the people, Be not ye afraid of them: remember the Lord, which is great and terrible, and fight for your brethren, your sons, and your daughters, your wives, and your houses." Nehemiah stood up and said, "We have to keep on building. We have to keep on battling. We can't focus on the rubbish."

It is the responsibility of the pastor to lift up the eyes of the people from all of the rubbish and problems and to get them to lift their eyes up to Jesus Christ. He must call them to a greater cause in life than bowling or softball.

Timothy Stackpole was a fire fighter with the New York City Fire Department. Not long before the terrorist attacks on New York City on September 11, 2001, he had rushed into a building fire and was terribly burned. For some time, his life hung in the balance. After many surgeries and extensive therapy, he finally came back to strength and desired to return to work.

In fact, in August of 2001, his superior officers came to him and encouraged him to take a desk job or an early retirement because the accident had lessened his mobility. After several meetings in which they tried to persuade him, Timothy told them, "I appreciate what you are asking me to do and what you are offering, but I have to go back to active duty. I have to go back. It is my calling to be a fireman."

He did go back. His first morning back to work was September 11. His first call was World Trade Center, Tower One. Timothy Stackpole gave his life that morning to save others.

What are you doing about your calling? If you were to win even one more soul by coming back to your true calling of reaching the lost, it would be worth it all.

In spite of discouragement and trials, Nehemiah was

persistent to His God-given calling! I challenge and encourage you to be faithful to the calling of Jesus Christ.

## Persistence When Tempted

Finally, Nehemiah was persistent when tempted to compromise. Time and time again the invitations came from Sanballat and Tobiah, calling Nehemiah away from the work, to the plain of Ono. This was a temptation in Nehemiah's life. The enemies of the work were trying to tempt Nehemiah into what we would call an "ecumenical gathering."

Today, there are those who say, "Believe in God all you want, and if you want to believe Jesus is God, that is fine: just put Him right here with Allah and Buddha and unknown gods. Just come along to our ministerial gathering and put aside the 'nonessentials' of Bible doctrine."

The Word of God is clear, "Come out from among them, and be ye separate." The Word of God is very clear that Jesus Christ is not to be on an equal plane, but that He is to have the preeminence. God has called us, not to hold hands with the worshippers of other gods, but He has called us to lift high the Lord Jesus Christ above all others!

71

Nehemiah was a man secure in his position and relationship with God. He was a man of discernment. He was a separated man with a purpose for living, and he was not going to come down from his God-given work in order to appease the enemy. He was going to stay at the work that God had given him to do.

If the Lord tarries in His coming much longer, America is headed for either anarchy or revival. There is no middle ground, just one way or the other. Many are questioning the possibility of revival. They base their views on the decaying of society and the lukewarmness of churches. Many church members and pastors would say it is impossible.

*America is headed for either anarchy or revival.*

Friend, there is hope for revival because our Anchor of hope is none other than the Rock Christ Jesus—Jesus Christ, the Rock; Jesus Christ, the Stone that was rejected; Jesus Christ, the Son of God! Jesus was crucified, yes, but thank God, He revived the Stone. Thank God that on the third day

> **Up from the grave He arose,**
> **With a mighty triumph o'er His foes.**

He arose a victor from the dark domain,
And He lives forever with His saints to reign.

Revival is possible because we serve a risen Saviour who has conquered death and Hell. He is the King of Kings and Lord of Lords, and He is coming again. If we would come back to the Word of God and the stones of prayer, purpose, and persistency, God could bless once again!

Think of it, "And without controversy great is the mystery of godliness: God was manifest in the flesh." He was not just another prophet, He was not just a lesser god, but God Himself was manifested in the flesh. He was "justified in the Spirit, seen of angels, preached unto the Gentiles, believed on in the world, received up into glory." I thank God that He is at the right hand of the Father. I thank God that I have an Intercessor and an Advocate. He is more interested in revival than all of our hearts could possibly comprehend.

When God called me to preach in 1975, I was so excited to be a part of the independent Baptist movement! I just could not wait! As God allowed me to get into the ministry, some reality checks came. Specifically, I remember two books I read in those days about church growth and church building. In 1972, the ten fastest-growing churches were independent Baptist. Eight of the ten largest churches were independent Baptist.

As I got involved in ministry, God called some of the great men home. Several of those once great men fell into sin. Others got discouraged and quit. Some say we got too involved in politics. I do not know exactly what happened; I just know it was not all that I thought it would be.

It is time that we say, "Lord, we believe there is something left to be done." It is time to humble ourselves and say, "God, I am willing to get down on my knees. I am willing to go to the rubbish pile and confess my sin and there find the stone of prayer. God, I will revive the stone of prayer. I will get prayer back into my life."

Through prayer God will revive the stone of purpose once again. May we say, "God, I will get back to winning souls. I will get back to loving my people. I will get back to doing what You called me to do."

Then, when the trials, discouragement, or ridicule comes, we will reach down for the stone of persistence. When the world's crowd calls, pick up that stone. When the discouragement comes, pick it up. We must want revival so badly, we will be willing to get down on our knees and find sweet communion in prayer with the Lord.

God can do it again. He is looking for people of faith. He is looking for a people who will revive the stones that He has blessed throughout all generations. May we have the purpose of Nehemiah in these last days. A right purpose will lead us to the path of revival.

# Setting the Course

1. During the time before Christ, what was probably one of the most devastating days in Jewish history?

   _____

   _____

   _____

2. As seen in the example of the story of Nehemiah, as soon as God's people determine to do something for the honor and glory of God, what quickly arises?

   _____

   _____

   _____

3. What are the three "stones" that need to be revived in fundamental churches today?

   _____

   _____

   _____

4. In Nehemiah 4, as he felt the burden for his people

and the city of Jerusalem, what was the first thing Nehemiah did?

_____

_____

_____

5. What would you say is the main thing that keeps Christians from a life of prayer? Is this true in your case?

_____

_____

_____

6. A closer look at the prayer of Nehemiah reveals what five qualities should be included in our prayer?

_____

_____

_____

7. According to Proverbs 28:13, what is the key to enabling God's work to go forward?

_____

_____

_____

8. When we pray in the way that the Word of God has dictated, what can we as Christians be assured of?

_____

_____

_____

9. The greater the prayer life, the clearer the vision and the stronger the motivation will be. What is your vision or motivation as a Christian?

_____

_____

_____

10. What are some things that could hinder the persistence of a Christian or ministry?

_____

_____

_____

## CHAPTER FOUR

# The Right Passion

## Having a Church That Pleases God

*"For yourselves, brethren, know our entrance in unto you, that it was not in vain: But even after that we had suffered before, and were shamefully entreated, as ye know, at Philippi, we were bold in our God to speak unto you the gospel of God with much contention. For our exhortation was not of deceit, nor of uncleanness, nor in guile: But as we were allowed of God to be put in trust with the gospel, even so we speak; not as pleasing men, but God, which trieth our hearts."*

I Thessalonians 2:1–4

Often in bookstores and libraries today we see books that deal with the subject of success. Titles can be found on how to be successful, how to get to the top, how to be a leader, or how to get rich quick. In America, it seems as if everyone wants to be successful. People want a successful church, a successful business, and a successful life. Desiring to be successful is not a wrong goal; however, success is a moving target; leadership is a fixed goal. If one really desires to be a spiritual leader in this day, he must make glorifying Jesus Christ his goal.

The goal of the church is to glorify the Lord Jesus Christ. In Matthew 5, the Bible declares that Christians are to be the salt and light of this world. Many in today's religious world believe that for a church to be successful, it must preach a less "salty" message and its light must not shine so boldly. This belief has placed the world's paradigm of success into our churches. God wants us to be successful only if we obey His Word and become the salt and the light of the world.

Charles Spurgeon, a great preacher of yesteryear, once said, "God, who is love, is first of all light; therefore, any thought of Him being soft or indulgent toward sin must be put away." Making the message of Christ soft to gain success as a church will please men but will not please God.

> *The goal of the church is to glorify the Lord Jesus Christ.*

The great first-century church of Thessalonica became a model church blessed by God. What was it about this church that made it successful in God's eyes? The Apostle Paul gave the Thessalonians some clear principles of what God considers true success. We can see the apostle's passion for God's work clearly in his ministry at Thessalonica.

## Paul Was Persistent in His Method

Paul begins this letter to the church with his testimony.

He reminds them of the trials he has faced since he began serving God; he reminds them also that through it all he remained faithful.

## Paul's Method at Philippi

In verses 1 and 2, he tells the church how he had been "shamefully entreated" at Philippi. The account of Paul's trip to Philippi can be found in Acts 16. The first lady saved in Philippi was Lydia. Paul then began to lead other people to Christ. The Bible records that during the fruitfulness of this ministry, the Apostle Paul was thrown into prison for preaching the Gospel of Jesus Christ.

## Paul's Method in Thessalonica

After Paul had been released from prison, he went to the next city, Thessalonica, and preached the same message with the same fervency. Christian, are you as persistent about the Gospel as Paul was? What causes you to stop witnessing for Jesus Christ?

Paul did not need to find a new seminar to teach him an easier way or a different style of witnessing. He only knew one style: to proclaim with boldness the Lord Jesus Christ, who was crucified and rose again for the sins of mankind.

Upon our move to Lancaster, I began knocking on doors and telling people about the Lord. After the first Sunday evening service, the bookkeeper came up to me and handed me a bank bag with the offering for the day. She said, "Pastor, this needs to be deposited at the bank."

Well, I do not recommend that the pastor be responsible for making the deposits, but apparently that was how it had been previously done. On Monday morning, I went to the bank with gospel tracts in my pocket. While standing in line I looked for opportunities to invite people to church. I eventually came to the window and handed the teller the money and deposit slip. I also handed her a tract and said, "My name is Paul Chappell, and I am the new pastor of Lancaster Baptist Church. I would like to invite you to come and visit our church sometime."

The teller immediately replied, "I know all about your church. Let me tell you something, mister: I bought the piano for that church, and no one ever gave me a thank-you note. No one ever said anything kind to me. People were mean to me at that church, and I will never go to that church again." I apologized to the teller and finished the transaction.

When I got back to the office later that afternoon from knocking on doors, the phone rang. The lady on the other end of the phone told me that my signature was not listed for the church's bank account, so I would need to come in as soon as possible to take care of it.

The next morning, I took some time to go by the bank. I went up to another window with a different lady and said, "I'm the new pastor at Lancaster Baptist Church. I need to fill out a signature card."

While she was finding the card, I pulled out a gospel tract and invited her to Lancaster Baptist Church. "We'd love to have you come and see what God is doing there," I told her.

She said, "I know all about that church! You people don't believe in speaking in tongues, and you know nothing about the Holy Spirit. The Holy Spirit helps you to speak in tongues, and until you speak in tongues I'm never coming to that church!"

Amazingly enough, the Holy Spirit also has something to do with producing the fruit of love, joy, and peace, which apparently she had not learned yet. After she read me the riot act about not having the Holy Spirit, I signed the signature card and left.

At the end of the Wednesday night service, we took up the offering, which meant on Thursday I had the "joy" of going back to the bank once again. I approached a different teller, gave her the bag, and pulled a gospel tract out of my pocket. I said, "Ma'am, I'd like to invite you to Lancaster Baptist Church. I'm the new pastor. I've just been in town a few days, and we'd sure love to have you come and visit us."

She said, "I'd never go to your church. Those two ladies over there told me about your church, and for an unkind, unloving man like you even to ask me is an insult." I quickly finished the deposit and went on my way.

When I got home that night after having spent the rest of the afternoon knocking on doors, I was a little discouraged. The first week of soulwinning had been seemingly unfruitful, and someone had broken into the church and stolen some things as well. It had just been a rough week. I got home on Thursday night, and my wife told me of the trouble she was having in getting the stores to take her out-of-town checks. She concluded that we needed to open a bank account.

I tried to persuade her that we really did not need a bank account, but she kept insisting that we did. I even tried to get her to do it some other time, but she pleaded her case well. Finally, I gave in and went to the bank the next day.

As I stood in line, I began to pray, "Lord, I've already talked to Ladies One, Two and Three, and they are not very interested, but if You would let me talk to someone else today, I'd be glad to do that."

By the grace and sovereignty of God, I went to a different lady on this particular day. As we began to fill out the paperwork for our family account, I took out a tract and invited her to be our guest at the Lancaster Baptist Church.

She said, "You know, last night my husband and I were saying that we needed to find a church." This lady and her husband came the very next Sunday, heard the Gospel preached, and walked down the aisle to accept Jesus Christ as their Saviour. On the same Sunday night, they were baptized.

I learned from this whole ordeal that persistence is rewarded when we keep our trust in God. Sometimes the door of opportunity swings on the hinges of opposition. On one occasion Spurgeon said that it was by perseverance that the snail reached the ark.

*It was by perseverance that the snail reached the ark.*

Christian, if you will just keep being persistent in biblical methods, God will be faithful. There may be trials along the way, but be faithful to get the message of God out to those who need to hear it.

# Paul Was Pure in His Motive

A passionate Christian will not only have persistent methods but will also have pure motives. In today's culture, great emphasis is placed on sincerity. People are looking for those who are pure in their motives. There are several things that can be noted about the Apostle Paul's motives.

### Not Deceitful

First of all, Paul was not a deceitful man. He said, "Our exhortation was not of deceit." In the city of Thessalonica, there were many types of temples and places of religious worship. These places were given over totally to idolatry. The temples of Zeus and Apollo were places of great sin and wickedness. The priests were known to be malicious and deceitful men, not interested in the spiritual welfare of the people. Paul makes a point of saying that his ministry was not one of deceit.

## Not Ego-centered

Second, Paul was not an ego-centered man. The Bible says in I Thessalonians 2:4, "But as we were allowed of God to be put in trust with the gospel, even so we speak; not as pleasing men, but God, which trieth our hearts." It was not Paul's desire to gain popularity with men, but rather to please God. He exemplified servant leadership by serving the Almighty God and the people of God.

The Bible says in Philippians 2:5–8, "Let this mind be in you, which was also in Christ Jesus: Who, being in the form of God, thought it not robbery to be equal with God: But made himself of no reputation, and took upon him the form of a servant, and was made in the likeness of men: And being found in fashion as a man, he humbled himself, and became obedient unto death, even the death of the cross."

This should be the mind of a mature Christian. It is a mind of humility and servitude, a mind that is willing to die to self and be alive to Christ. Our motivation for service should be our love for the Lord and the desire to glorify Him.

## Not Covetous

Paul's motivation was neither man's recognition, nor was

it self-gratification. In I Thessalonians 2:5 the Bible says, "For neither at any time used we flattering words, as ye know, nor a cloke of covetousness; God is witness."

In today's society, people are suspicious of the motives of Christian servants, pastors, deacons, evangelists, and church members. Paul was not looking for a handout, nor was he looking for his needs and wants to be provided by those he served.

In my own life, I have found that if I am faithful to the Word of God, He will meet every need in my life. There is no need for covetousness. God is a God who loves us and will abundantly supply for us.

In the early days of our church I received no salary. My wife and I were living by faith and trusting God to provide. One Sunday evening after about two weeks of living in Lancaster, my wife told me there were no groceries in the house and we really did not have the money to purchase more. After church that night, we were invited to go with some of our church members to a little Mexican restaurant called Naugles.

As we headed toward the restaurant, I asked my wife, "Sweetheart, do you have any money that we might buy some food tonight?"

She said, "Honey, I don't have any money." Now, I do not know how it is in your home, but when my wife says she does not have any money, she normally has twenty dollars in the bottom of her purse she does not know about!

I replied, "Sweetheart, I know you don't have any money, but give me some money!"

She got big tears in her eyes and said, "Not only do I not have any money, but we're out of food. I'm not sure how we're going to feed our family tomorrow."

We began to dig in the seats to get all of the loose change from the back seat, but it was only enough to buy a drink. As we approached the counter and started to order a drink, the employee said to me, "Sir, we just had a vanload of teenagers drive through and order all these bags of food and drive off as a joke. We're just going to have to throw the food away. If you would like to have it, we'd be glad to give it to you to eat tonight."

My wife and I looked at each other, cried and hugged and gave each other "high fives." We went over to the corner and thought about how good God had been to us as we ate that food.

That next morning there was a knock at the door of our home. On the other side stood a pastor friend from near

San Diego, California. He said, "Brother Chappell, I don't really know why, but last night during the middle of our service, God burdened my heart for you and your family. We took an offering for your family, drove to a twenty-four-hour grocery store, and bought these groceries for you and your family." They brought us enough groceries to eat for several weeks.

> *What a tragedy today that the average Christian is hiding the light of the Gospel!*

When you are in the center of God's will and your motives are right and pure before Him, God will take care of you. This is proven time and time again in the Word of God.

What was Paul's goal in life? What was he after? It can be summed up in verse 4: "But as we were allowed of God to be put in trust with the gospel, even so we speak; not as pleasing men, but God, which trieth our hearts." Paul's motive was to be a good steward of the Gospel. First Corinthians 4:2 states, "Moreover it is required in stewards, that a man be found faithful." God's will is very clear for our lives.

When He saved us, God gave us a wonderful message,

and we are to be good stewards of that message. God does not want our light to be hidden. What a tragedy today that the average Christian is hiding the light of the Gospel!

# Paul Was Personal in His Ministry

The third characteristic necessary in real ministry is the personal touch. First Thessalonians 2:7 states, "But we were gentle among you, even as a nurse cherisheth her children." The Apostle Paul reveals his heart through this verse.

## Personal in His Care

First of all, he was personal in his care, like a nursing mother would be. He loved people with a special love. All around us in the community are men and women whose families are falling apart. People who have made a lot of money are still sad, sorrowful, and lonely. There are those who are in convalescent hospitals and those who are drunken or filled with dope who need the love of Jesus Christ!

Oh, that we would be as gentle as a nursing mother giving the milk of the Word, as patient as a loving parent. Working with people does require patience. No one

93

develops overnight the distinctiveness and maturity of one who has walked with Jesus and been filled with the Spirit of God for many years. As Christians, we need to make the church a place where people can feel and know the love of Jesus Christ while we still hold to biblical doctrine and an uncompromising stand.

Laura was saved many years ago in our church while in her seventies. It is not a normal thing for someone to be saved that late in life. There were many habits in her life that just were not being broken overnight. She could curse up a blue streak, and every once in a while she described in a very unique way how my message blessed her.

She was a chain smoker and would go gambling quite a bit. One day she came forward at the invitation and said, "Pastor, I'm here tonight to do whatever you want me to do. I believe God wants me to serve Him, and I'm here to say I want to serve the Lord."

I began thinking about it. I knew she was not ready to teach a fifth-grade girls' Sunday school class. God gave me a moment of inspiration, and I said, "Laura, I know just what you can do. You can be in charge of the vacuum ministry." She did the best job anyone has ever done vacuuming the church. She not only vacuumed the church, but she also took the vacuums to the vacuum shop to have the belts and bags replaced. She was just so excited to serve God!

At that time we were buying the land where our church now sits and were involved in a campaign to raise funds. We had a board up in front of the church with twenty different squares, each square representing an acre of land that we needed to buy. As the money was raised, we would fill in those squares. It was a time of faith and sacrifice.

One day Laura walked into my office with an envelope for me. She wanted me to open it. I replied, "Oh, I don't need to do that, Laura. I'll just give it to the bookkeeper." She kept insisting that I open it, and being afraid that she would start cursing, I went ahead and opened it.

In the envelope were five brand-new one-hundred-dollar bills. She said, "Pastor, I've been playing bingo for a long time, but I didn't start winning until I got saved."

You say, "Well, Brother Chappell, did you exegete the Scriptures to her and help her to understand the evils of gambling?" No, I prayed that she would keep on winning because we were trying to buy property and build the building!

All joking aside, sometimes it takes some patience working with people. Actually, as we taught Laura and she matured in the Lord, she grew out of some of those things. A loving church and church family are the kind that can meet people where they are. Paul was personal in his care and in his commitment.

Paul did not just stand up and read a Sunday school quarterly on Sunday morning. "So being affectionately desirous of you, we were willing to have imparted unto you, not the gospel of God only, but also our own souls, because ye were dear unto us" (I Thessalonians 2:8). The Apostle Paul shared his life and his heart. He poured himself into people to help meet their needs.

It has often been stated that people do not care how much you know until they know how much you care.

*People do not care how much you know until they know how much you care.*

The neighbor next door does not care about how separated you are or how dogmatically you can defend the Scriptures. He wants to know if you can come pray for him right now because his wife has just left him or if you can come pray with her because she was just diagnosed with cancer. Your neighbor just wants to know if you will be his friend. It is critically important that as a Christian you do not neglect the personal touch.

## Paul Was Powerful in His Message

While the Apostle Paul was persistent in his methods, pure in his motives, and personal in his ministry, he did not neglect the most important thing, a powerful message. Notice in I Thessalonians 2:9: "For ye remember, brethren, our labour and travail: for labouring night and day, because we would not be chargeable unto any of you, we preached unto you the gospel of God."

The Apostle Paul preached the Gospel of Jesus Christ. Verse 13 says, "For this cause also thank we God without ceasing, because, when ye received the word of God which ye heard of us, ye received it not as the word of men, but as it is in truth, the word of God, which effectually worketh also in you that believe."

This is a bold assertion of the fact that what Paul was giving to them was not his opinion nor his ideas, but the very Word of God. God's Holy Spirit breathed His words through this man and then preserved them down through the years for us. Paul said his message was not of himself but was the Gospel of Christ, the Word of God.

What a wonderful blessing to know that now, some two thousand years later, we as Christians are still hearing the same message in the same way—the same Gospel, the same Jesus, the same Word of God preached.

Jesus said, "Man shall not live by bread alone, but by every word that proceedeth out of the mouth of God." It is a powerful, life-changing message. The Bible says in Romans 1:16, "For I am not ashamed of the gospel of Christ: for it is the power of God unto salvation to every one that believeth; to the Jew first, and also to the Greek." "For the word of God is quick, and powerful, and sharper than any twoedged sword, piercing even to the dividing asunder of soul and spirit, and of the joints and marrow, and is a discerner of the thoughts and intents of the heart" (Hebrews 4:12).

The Bible says that this Word pierces "even to the dividing asunder of soul and spirit." The Word of God will do what music, counseling, psychology, or propaganda cannot do! The ability for lives to change today is found in the power and authority of the Word of God. That is why Paul said to Timothy in II Timothy 4:2, "Preach the word; be instant in season, out of season; reprove, rebuke, exhort with all longsuffering and doctrine."

I have never failed to be in awe as I have watched the

Gospel change someone's life.

I remember going out soulwinning one particular Saturday with my daughter, Danielle. We followed up on a particular family that had visited our church a few weeks prior. As we knocked on the door, I could hear loud rock music playing. The door was opened, and the lady invited us to come in. We went in, sat on the couch, and I began to discuss the church with her and her husband.

After a little while, the lady turned the rock music off. I began to talk to the husband. He had long hair and a couple of earrings and just looked rough. I asked him, "Sir, if you were to die today, do you know for sure that Heaven would be your home? Would you go to Heaven? Would you go to Hell? Or do you know?"

He said, "You know, I've been thinking about that very issue. I'm not sure that I really know where I would go."

I said, "Would you mind if I took the next few moments to show you how you could know for sure that Heaven is your home?"

He said, "I'd like that very much."

About thirty minutes later he prayed and accepted Jesus

99

Christ as his personal Saviour. That next Sunday he and his wife came and identified with the Lord in believer's baptism. Sunday night they came to church. After the service was over, as we gathered out in the lobby, I talked with him and asked, "Joe, would you like to come with me tomorrow night? I'll be preaching down in the Los Angeles area, and I'd love to have you travel with me there. You can hear some of the songs and the preaching and get a feel for the Christian life."

He said, "You want me to go with you to another church?"

I said, "Sure, Joe, I'd love to have you go with me."

Well, he said he'd like to go, and I agreed to pick him up at about five o'clock the next afternoon. I pulled up in front of his house and saw a man I did not recognize come through the doorway. Where the earrings had been, there were no earrings. He had on a three-piece suit and had gotten a sharp haircut.

As he got into the car he said, "Hi, Pastor. I got a new Bible today. It's the King George Version. Did I get the right one?"

How did his life take such change? It was by the power of the Gospel of Jesus Christ, by the presence of the Holy Spirit of God. People that you think are beyond hope are not beyond hope. The people you think cannot be reached, can be reached by the power of the Gospel of Jesus Christ.

What does God consider a successful Christian or a successful church? One that lifts up the light of the glorious Gospel so men and women might be saved and so lives might be changed for the glory of God. May God use all of us to serve Him with the

*A successful Christian lifts up the light of the glorious Gospel.*

right passion in this day. Let us remember to follow a biblical pathway and pattern for ministry even as the Apostle Paul modeled in Thessalonica.

# Setting the Course

1. Since success is often a moving target and leadership, a fixed goal, for a spiritual leader what must be the goal?

   _____

   _____

   _____

2. It is easy to find churches in today's society changing the message to accommodate men. What are some of the ways that this message has changed?

   _____

   _____

   _____

3. When an unsaved person comes in contact with Christians and the church ministry, what are some of the characteristics of that ministry that are being evaluated? These characteristics are mentioned specifically in I Thessalonians 2:1–4.

   _____

   _____

   _____

4. Why should there be no need for covetousness in the Christian's life?

_____

_____

_____

5. In I Thessalonians 2:7, Paul wrote, "But we were gentle among you, even as a nurse cherisheth her children." In other words, working with people in the ministry will require what?

_____

_____

_____

6. When an unsaved person comes to church, what should he feel from the members and people in ministry? _____

   In other words, people do not care how much you _____ until they know how much you _____.

7. However, although having personal ministry is important in making people feel like they can be a

part, it is also vitally important that what not be compromised in the process?

_____

_____

_____


8. Write out one verse that emphasizes the importance of having the right message in our churches.

_____

_____

_____

## CHAPTER FIVE

# The Right Doctrine

## Standing Strong Upon the Word of God

*"Hear, ye children, the instruction of a father, and attend to know understanding. For I give you good doctrine, forsake ye not my law. For I was my father's son, tender and only beloved in the sight of my mother. He taught me also, and said unto me, Let thine heart retain my words: keep my commandments, and live."*

Proverbs 4:1–4

W**hen** reading the Book of Proverbs, we are reading more than a collection of sayings from Solomon to Rehoboam. We are truly studying the principles of the Holy Spirit of God and declarations from God the Father to each of His children.

In Proverbs 4:2 God says, "I give you good doctrine...." Webster defines *doctrine* as a set of beliefs. Through His Word, God is giving us a set of beliefs by which to live. Doctrine is what brings us together. Doctrine is the glue that holds us together within the local church. Every church must have proper doctrine to be a true New Testament church.

"All scripture is given by inspiration of God, and is profitable for doctrine, for reproof, for correction, for instruction in righteousness" (II Timothy 3:16). A true church believes that the Bible is the infallible, inerrant Word of God. A true church believes in the deity of Jesus Christ and that He is the eternally preexistent Son

*Doctrine is the glue that holds us together within the local church.*

of God. A true church believes in the depravity of man and in the blood atonement of Jesus Christ for our salvation.

Without true doctrine, you may have a building but not a church. We must recognize the importance of doctrine. Every biblical church must have true doctrine.

Not only must every church be built on biblical doctrine, but every home should be built on solid Bible doctrine. A strong home recognizes the headship of Christ. A strong home is where mother and father daily gather the children around the Word of God and instruct them in the ways of God. In a strong home a man looks and acts like a man, and a lady looks and acts like a lady. In a strong home there is more love for the local church than television. They find themselves faithfully following the Word of God. Thank God for men today who say, "As for me and my house, we will serve the Lord." A strong home is built on strong doctrine.

In America, many professing Christians are showing a great disdain for doctrine. They are criticizing the uplifting of doctrine. They are saying that doctrine is not necessary for today. The cry of the ecumenical movement tells us to tear down the walls of doctrine and denominationalism.

While there is nothing sacred about a denomination, there is something very sacred about the doctrine that is often being dismissed as "nonessential" in Christendom. Without an adherence to doctrine, we have no true unity. Pure doctrine is not from man but from God.

# The Priority of Good Doctrine

It is the will of God that you and I hold to good doctrine. It is not to be forsaken. As Joshua raised the twelve stones at Gilgal as a testimony to the power and the presence of God, we are commanded not to remove the "ancient landmarks." The New Testament teaches us that the church is to be the pillar and ground of the truth. We are to raise the truth up for a lost and dying world.

For these many years here in Lancaster, California, we have conducted a new members' reception about every six weeks. In recent years, I have met with thirty to fifty new adult members to share with them a little about the history of the church. I talk to them about our Baptist distinctives, the program of the church, what the church believes, and some truths about the fundamental doctrines of the Word of God.

Some people may be surprised that we teach this to the brand-new members of our church as they are being assimilated into our fellowship. We want to be honest about the fact that we are old-fashioned, Bible-believing Christians who believe in the doctrines of the Word of God.

God says we are to hold to the doctrine and not forsake it. The Scriptures also show that we are to honor the doctrine of the Word of God.

"Get wisdom, get understanding: forget it not; neither decline from the words of my mouth. Forsake her not, and she shall preserve thee: love her, and she shall keep thee. Wisdom is the principal thing; therefore get wisdom: and with all thy getting get understanding" (Proverbs 4:5–7). "The fear of the LORD is the beginning of knowledge" (Proverbs 1:7).

A man some years ago said to me, "Well, Brother Chappell, I believe that the fear of man bringeth a snare. No man is going to tell me where I can preach and how I should behave in my ministry."

I replied, "The fear of man may bring a snare, but do not forget that the fear of the Lord is the beginning of wisdom."

Rather than being reactionary and running away from what we think some other man thinks, we need to be thinking about what God thinks. "Take heed unto thyself, and unto the doctrine; continue in them: for in doing this thou shalt both save thyself, and them that hear thee" (I Timothy 4:16).

Several years ago my wife and I were in the state of Vermont, where I had the opportunity to preach for a few days. During one of our free afternoons, we drove down to a riverside area and saw a beautiful old Congregational church. We are not used to a lot of the New England type of scenery, so we went inside the church and looked at the old pews and architecture.

After awhile an elderly man came into the auditorium. I introduced myself and told him I was a pastor from California. He introduced himself as the pastor of the church.

I said, "Sir, this is a beautiful church. I have read much

about the Congregational churches of the last century. I would like to know a little bit about this church. How do you approach the Word of God? What kind of convictions do you have about the Bible?"

I will never forget what he said: "We approach the Bible as a very inspirational book. The Bible is a book that inspires me." (By the way, that's the classic answer of a liberal. The Bible is not merely inspiring; it is the inspired Word of God!) He continued to say, "Personally, I like the Gospel of Mark. It affects me, but I really do not enjoy the Gospel of John as much. I tend to question some portions of it."

As he spoke, I was reminded of what it says in James 1:8: "A double minded man is unstable in all his ways." There is a story told of a group of soldiers preparing to go into the heat of battle the next day. One young soldier went to his buddy, handed him a letter, and said, "If I do not make it back, I would like you to give this letter to Sally. Tell her my thoughts were of her and that her name was the last word that came from my lips. Also, here is a letter for Helen. Tell her the same thing."

Taking the approach that some of the Word of God is inspired and some of it is not is both the greatest injustice and spiritual adultery. All of the Bible is the Word of God, which was inspired by the Holy Spirit and preserved for us until this day.

# The Pathway of Good Doctrine

"I have taught thee in the way of wisdom; I have led thee in right paths" (Proverbs 4:11). The right doctrine will provide the right pathway for your life.

### The Right Direction

When we moved to Lancaster, California, we established some things in the church to which we would hold fast and be faithful. We established that it would be a soulwinning church. We established this church to be sound in doctrine. We established that this church would have godly music and a missions program.

We had no salary or ministry program in those days, but we had doctrine. The right kind of doctrine will provide the right direction and the right pathway in our lives, but that direction is not always appreciated.

*The right doctrine will provide the right pathway for your life.*

On one occasion a man questioned me about our

position on certain issues. The issue of homosexuality came up, and we shared with him what the Bible teaches on that issue. That Sunday night a fax came into our fax machine threatening our family for my preaching of the Word of God on this particular area.

During one of our early staff meetings, we were discussing some of the doctrines of the church. One staff member asked, "Pastor, what do we say to those who are wanting to join the church but are living together outside of marriage?"

I said, "Well, I do not know. I suppose we had better be patient with putting them in the church membership until they make the right decision." This was somewhat of an easy thing to discuss in the staff meeting.

That next Sunday morning a big tall man came forward with a tiny lady beside him. He shook my hand and said, "We are here to join the church."

I gave him over to the man who had asked the question in the staff meeting and said, "These folks would like to become members of our church." I thought that was that. We do it all the time.

After the service, I was standing in the foyer. This big tall man came up to me and said, "Listen, that man over there said I cannot join your church just because me and the little lady are living together and have never been married. That really bothers me. I was a member of another Baptist church, and my tithe check cashes just like anybody else's tithe check."

I said, "Well, sir, we are really not trying to offend you. We are just trying to be true to what we believe the Word of God teaches."

He began to curse and yell. Some of the men of the church got between us, and I found myself going around the corner and out to the side of the parking lot! My family was already by the car. As I put my hand on the door handle, I looked down the side of the church and saw this guy running full-steam toward me. I tried to get in the car as quickly as I could but did not make it.

He came up to me, grabbed my arm, looked me in the eye and said, "You are right! We have been saying for years we ought to get married. You are right!" A few days later, they did get married. The right doctrine establishes the right direction for your ministry and helps you know the way of God.

**The Right Assurance**
Right doctrine provides not only the right direction but

also the right assurance in your life. "When thou goest, thy steps shall not be straitened; and when thou runnest, thou shalt not stumble" (Proverbs 4:12).

This old-fashioned pathway of doctrine is a proven pathway. You will find that the Lord Jesus Christ has smoothed out this old-fashioned pathway of doctrine. God has already prepared the way for you. Solid footing will be found in following the right doctrine.

Jeremiah 6:16 says, "Thus saith the LORD, Stand ye in the ways, and see, and ask for the old paths, where is the good way, and walk therein, and ye shall find rest for your souls."

"Who is wise, and he shall understand these things? prudent, and he shall know them? for the ways of the LORD are right, and the just shall walk in them: but the transgressors shall fall therein" (Hosea 14:9).

*Stand in the pathway of fundamental truth.* Dr. Curtis Hutson wrote me a letter in September of 1994. The closing portion read, "Paul, I challenge you to stand in the long line of independent fundamental Baptists who have stood for soulwinning and separation." Though Dr. Hutson's body was already filled with cancer, he was challenging me as a young preacher to stand in the pathway that is guarded by the doctrine of the Word of God. Stand in the pathway of fundamental truth.

## The Provision of Good Doctrine

"But the path of the just is as the shining light, that shineth more and more unto the perfect day" (Proverbs 4:18).

Along this pathway of good doctrine shines the glorious light of the Gospel of Christ. This pathway is illuminated by the Scriptures. Good doctrine lifts up the light of the Gospel of Jesus. "In him was life; and the life was the light of men" (John 1:4).

One of the reasons I thank God for our Bible-preaching churches is that, for the most part, they are still taking the light of the Gospel into every community. It may not be the broadest path nor the most popular path, but it is the path where Jesus walks.

Not long ago, my wife and I went on a vacation with our family. One evening we asked the kids if they would mind staying in the hotel room while my wife and I went out for a date. We ordered pizza for them and let them spend some time together.

After Terrie and I had a nice dinner together, we walked into a gift store that also sold Thomas Kinkade paintings. We were observing these beautiful paintings when a young man named Todd, a basketball player for Colorado State University, told us he was working there for the summer. As we talked, I told him where we were from and that I was a pastor. He said to me, "You know, my grandmother was a Christian, but she died a few months ago." When he referred to this, I saw his countenance fall.

I said, "Todd, the Bible tells how you can know for sure that one day you will be in Heaven and not only see your grandmother but the Lord Jesus Christ Himself. Would you allow me a few moments to show you how you can know for sure that one day Heaven will be your home?"

In the midst of that busy art gallery and gift shop, we sat down on a little couch with beautiful paintings all around us. On the opposite side of me was a beautiful painting of the cross, with spotlights on it.

I talked to Todd about his need as a sinner and told him how much Christ loved him. As I shared the Word of God with him, one of his co-workers, a Christian whom we had met two days before, came in, slipped a Bible into my hands, and shut the door of the room. I told Todd how Jesus died on the cross for his sin and that by accepting Christ as Saviour, he could one day be in Heaven.

After a short time, he prayed and accepted Christ as his Saviour. He looked up after he had finished praying and said, "I want to ask you a question. Is the verse at the corner of this painting the one I see a lot in gymnasiums at basketball games?"

I asked, "Do you mean John 3:16?"

He said, "That is the one. How does that go?"

As I quoted the verse, that six-foot-five basketball player began to cry. He said, "I've seen that John 3:16 in gymnasiums and football stadiums, but it did not mean a thing to me until right now when I accepted Christ."

I thank God for churches that lift high the doctrine of soulwinning. Churches that do not emphasize this matter of strong Bible doctrine are not seeing souls saved. You may see advertisements telling of their growth, but they are not growing according to Acts 2:47: "And the Lord added to the church daily such as should be saved."

My friend, there is a certain type of church growth that does not use that word *saved.* I am not interested in that kind of growth. I do not believe the Lord is either. The pathway of good doctrine is illuminated with the light of salvation. Thank God that the glorious gospel light is still shining and souls are still being saved!

> *The pathway of good doctrine is illuminated with the light of salvation.*

Someone may ask, "How can you continue going out soulwinning and witnessing?" We have the words that will save a man's soul and change his eternal destiny. As long as there are the doctrines of Heaven, Hell, and salvation, we need to stay on the soulwinning path.

During one of our singles' summer retreats, we took our group up to the beautiful Yosemite National Park. As I came in for one of evening services, one of the men told me a story about something that had just taken place in the park.

There was a group of handicapped children who had come to Yosemite with a doctor from Los Angeles. During the previous months of schooling, the children had studied about Yosemite and its beauty. They began to dream of someday being able to hike up the trail of Bridal Veil Falls to see some of the park's beauty.

The doctor eventually was able to take them to this particular trail to fulfill their dream. As they began to climb the trail, it was very difficult for them. In fact, they were inching their way along.

As the children were making their way up this trail, the basketball team from UCLA ran past the children to the mountaintop in preparation for their season. As these tall, physically fit, young men went by the children, the doctor saw what little hope the youngsters had left fall from their faces. They persisted on but even more slowly than before.

About an hour later, the men came running down the trail. Instead of continuing to the bottom, each man picked up one of the handicapped children, put him on his back, and ran him all the way to the top of the mountain. After the children were able to take in the spectacular sight, the men carried them down to the bottom of the mountain. Later that night, the basketball team came and spent time with the children around the campfire.

After hearing this story, I began to think about the fact

that there was a day when I was traveling along a pathway called Sin. As I inched my way to nowhere, Jesus came and picked me up out of the miry clay and set my feet upon the rock of salvation.

Because of salvation, Christ not only saves us, but He comes to fellowship with us on a daily basis. Throughout the course of life, He guides us with the light of His wonderful Word.

As a leader, you may hear about other places that do not hold to the same doctrine as you, yet they are growing. Do not question the doctrines and standards in your life. Remember, never doubt in the night what God gave you in the light. If He gave you a conviction on a certain doctrine, stand on that doctrine. "Hold fast the form of sound words, which thou hast heard of me, in faith and love which is in Christ Jesus" (II Timothy 1:13). Be true to the Lord and His doctrine.

I find in these days many men who once made a decision about soulwinning but are now saying, "I see the landmark, and I know what I once said. I am just going to take this landmark and move it back over here for a while. I am not sure that that is what I really want to do with my life."

God's Word, the doctrinal Book, will help you and guide your path.

Pastors today are going to seminars to learn some different ways about growing a church. They are being taught that some doctrines and standards are not necessary anymore. If you let church growth become your god, you will change every doctrine.

> *If you let church growth become your god, you will change every doctrine.*

Oh, that preachers today would get back to the old Book and the way God has chosen for His people to follow! Preachers need to give the glory back to God once again. Those who have spent too much of their time running around with the wrong crowd and walking down the wrong pathway need to come back to the old-fashioned, Bible-believing fundamentalism that has been proven and tested by time and eternity.

Paul said to Timothy, "Preach the word; be instant in season, out of season; reprove, rebuke, exhort with all longsuffering and doctrine" (II Timothy 4:2).

God says, "I give you good **doctrine.**" May we get a

hold of biblical doctrine and follow its right pathway in our everyday living!

# Setting the Course

1. Proverbs 4:2 mentions, "I give you good doctrine...."
   What is doctrine? and what does it mean for the
   believer?

   _____

   _____

   _____

2. Biblical doctrine is the cornerstone for many things
   in the Christian life. What are a few?

   _____

   _____

   _____

3. How does the religious realm, especially the ecumenical movement, feel about doctrine today?

   _____

   _____

   _____

4. What does biblical doctrine provide for the church?

   _____

   _____

   _____

5. Write out I Timothy 4:16.

   _____

   _____

   _____

6. According to Proverbs 4:12, right doctrine provides not only the right direction in life but also what?

   _____

   _____

   _____

7. When evaluating doctrine, how can a Christian tell if what is being taught is good doctrine?

   _____

   _____

   _____

8. Proverbs 4:18 states, "But the path of the just is as the shining light, that shineth more and more unto the perfect day." What "light" does good doctrine reveal?

_____

_____

_____

## CHAPTER SIX

# The Right Priorities

## Understanding the Biblical Priorities
## of Ministry

*"For the love of Christ constraineth us; because we thus judge, that if one died for all, then were all dead: And that he died for all, that they which live should not henceforth live unto themselves, but unto him which died for them, and rose again. Wherefore henceforth know we no man after the flesh: yea, though we have known Christ after the flesh, yet now henceforth know we him no more. Therefore if any man be in Christ, he is a new creature: old things are passed away; behold, all things are become new. And all things are of God, who hath reconciled us to himself by Jesus Christ, and hath given to us the ministry of reconciliation; To wit, that God was in Christ, reconciling the world unto himself, not imputing their trespasses unto them; and hath committed unto us the word of reconciliation. Now then we are ambassadors for Christ, as though God did beseech you by us: we pray you in Christ's stead, be ye reconciled to God. For he hath made him to be sin for us, who knew no sin; that we might be made the righteousness of God in him."*

II Corinthians 5:14–21

Let me draw your attention to the phrase "and hath given to us the ministry of reconciliation." There are some Christians who have come to the place where they realize that life is more than being a nurse, a doctor, a carpenter, a police officer, or an aerospace worker. When someone is saved, God gives him a new purpose for living and a new career, to do the work of the Lord Jesus Christ.

## First Imperative

It is obvious that the life of the Apostle Paul included two great motivating factors that kept him going in the Christian life. These two biblical imperatives gripped his soul and constantly reminded him of what life was all about as a Christian. The first imperative was that

Paul never got over the fact that the Son of God had per-

> *God gives a new purpose and a new career, to do the work of the Lord Jesus Christ.*

sonally died on the cross for his sin. He says in verse 14, "For the love of Christ constraineth us...."

Undoubtedly, there are people who have gotten over it. There was once a time when their lives were lived for Christ, but now the focus has become pleasure or a career. No longer is there a compulsion from within to serve with joy. It has become mundane. If that is where you are, you should ask the Lord, as the psalmist once did, to restore the joy of your salvation.

Paul's life never failed to reflect the joy he still had for his salvation. He was compelled to hazard himself, because he loved Jesus Christ. He never felt as though he had to do certain things. He just had a desire for the Lord Jesus Christ. An understanding of God's love and grace had not caused him to live carelessly but to live very zealously for the Lord Jesus Christ.

Do you remember the day you were saved? Maybe one reason people do not have the joy of the Lord is that they never got saved in the first place.

# Second Imperative

Another thing Paul never got over was that once he had been saved, God had given him a personal ministry. God gave him a reason for living. If all we have to live for is a job or possessions, we are living for ourselves. This becomes a very empty life.

When someone accepts Jesus Christ as Saviour, he has something really big to live for in the Lord Jesus Christ. That is what Paul is talking about when the Spirit of the Lord inspires him in verse 18 to say, "…and hath given to us the ministry of reconciliation."

Have you come to the place in your life where you have recognized that God has given you the ministry of reconciliation? I am afraid that many Christians have forgotten their purpose for being born again. It is not merely to get fire insurance out of Hell. Our purpose should be to glorify Christ by letting Him work in us and through us.

I once heard of a primary-age girl who would go to school every day trying to be important by having special things in her purse. She kept Kleenex and other small things that she had gathered from her house, and yet the other girls at school always seemed to have more important things in their purses.

One day after school, she decided that she was going to get some really important things to put in her purse. She went to her mother's desk and began to look around. As she began to put things like pens and pencils into her purse, a document caught her attention. It looked important, and she could read her name on it. It was her birth certificate. Folding it up, she put it in her purse to show her friends at school.

The next day as she walked to school, she opened her purse to make sure the certificate was still there. She was so excited to show her friends at recess! While she was looking at her birth certificate, a gust of wind blew it out of her hand. She chased it across the parking lot. The faster she ran, the further away it seemed to blow ahead of her. Finally, the wind lifted it up and took it over the fence of the school playground. She stood at the fence and began to cry. After a little while, the school janitor came over to her and asked her why she was crying. Despairingly, she looked up at the man and

> *The priority of the ministry is the Word of God.*

said, "I just lost my excuse for being born!"

I am afraid that many Christians have lost their excuse for being born again. They have forgotten the reason that they were saved in the first place. Paul never forgot the reason he was born again!

# The Priority of Ministry

We have seen that Paul never forgot his calling. In verse 18, we see Paul's presentation of the priority of ministry: "And all things are of God, who hath reconciled us to himself by Jesus Christ, and hath given to us the ministry of reconciliation."

### The Word of God

The Bible teaches that there is a priority of ministry. Notice verse 19: "To wit, that God was in Christ, reconciling the world unto himself, not imputing their trespasses unto them; and hath committed unto us the word of reconciliation." The priority of the ministry is the Word of God. If you are saved and want to be involved in ministry, you must recognize that the priority of the ministry is not a broom, a towel, or a basketball; the priority in ministry always revolves around the Word of God. There is no real ministry happening without the

Word of God. The church is the pillar and ground of truth. We are not here to lift up primarily some social cause or banner of this world. We exist to lift up the Word of God, which is the priority of the church.

In this day, people call everything within the church a ministry. They have this idea that they can be involved in Christian service and call that ministry. Although we have sometimes associated cleaning and cooking around church as a ministry in the past, they are really acts of service. The word "ministry" in the New Testament means to serve or aid as a Christian teacher. The priority of the ministry revolves around the teaching of the Word of God. When you study the word "ministry" in the Bible, you find it is speaking about sharing the Word of God— transferring the Word of God from one person to another. Many Christians are doing good deeds, but these good works have become a "novocaine" to their soul and a substitute for the fact that they are not actually involved in sharing the Bible with other people.

> *Good works have become a substitute for sharing the Bible with others.*

Sometimes fathers and mothers are not teaching the

Word of God to their own children, much less being involved in soulwinning and witnessing. Paul says in Acts 21:19, "And when he had saluted them, he declared particularly what things God had wrought among the Gentiles by his ministry." First Timothy 1:12 says, "And I thank Christ Jesus our Lord, who hath enabled me, for that he counted me faithful, putting me into the ministry." The Word of God also says in Acts 20:24, "But none of these things move me, neither count I my life dear unto myself, so that I might finish my course with joy, and the ministry, which I have received of the Lord Jesus, to testify the gospel of the grace of God." Paul says that his ministry was to testify of the Gospel of the grace of God. Acts 6:4 says, "But we will give ourselves continually to prayer, and to the ministry of the word." The priority of the ministry revolves around the teaching and sharing of the Word of God. My dream is to see church members as growing ministers of the Word of God by faithfully leading others to Christ. I would like to see members be able to take the Word of God and show others the assurance of salvation and the truths of God's Word.

You do not have to sign up to be a teacher to teach this blessed Book to other people. Ephesians 4:11 says, "And he gave some, apostles; and some, prophets; and some, evangelists; and some, pastors and teachers." The "he" in verse 11 is Jesus Christ, the Head of the church. He gives a pastor to the church "for the perfecting of the saints" (Ephesians 4:12). The word "perfecting" means "maturing" or "development." God gives a pastor to the church to help in the maturing of the church so the whole church can be involved in the work of the ministry. The word "ministry" here is not in the context of general service, but it is in the context of the ministry of the Word of God. The only way that the local body of Christ is going to be edified is through the teaching and preaching of the Word of God. We all need to recognize that the priority of the ministry is the Word of God.

True discipleship always involves aiding other people in the Word of God. We can serve God in many ways that do not require an understanding of the Bible at all. For example, we can clean, organize, and even sing. Real ministry involves the transferring of the Word of God. Ministry is really alive when everyone in the church is involved in someone else's life. Do not think I am belittling the need for Christian service. I thank the Lord for Christian servants who would clean, help, and serve. Yet we must be aware of the fact that God is calling us to be in the ministry and the priority of the ministry is the teaching of the Word of God. Paul said in II Cor-

138

inthians 4: "Therefore seeing we have this ministry, as we have received mercy, we faint not." Paul's understanding of ministry was that when he was saved, God also called him into the ministry. At Lancaster Baptist we often say, "Every member a minister," and we are saying that every member ought to know how to lead someone else to Christ. The priority of the ministry is the Word of God.

## The Word of Reconciliation

The priority of the ministry is specifically tied to the Word of reconciliation. The priority of the ministry is the Word of God, but the theme of the Bible is the reconciliation of a lost world to God through Jesus Christ. In verse 19 Paul says, "To wit, that God was in Christ, reconciling the world unto himself, not imputing their trespasses unto them; and hath committed unto us the word of reconciliation."

*The theme of the Bible is the reconciliation of a lost world to God through Jesus Christ.*

This verse is stating that God was in Christ. Think of the ramifications of that—God was in Christ! No, Jesus is not just another god or another prophet; Jesus Christ truly is the Son of God. The Bible says God was in Christ and Jesus Christ came that the world might be saved. He came to seek and to save the lost, but now He has given us the ministry of reconciliation.

When Christ called the disciples to Himself, He was calling out the first church. Shortly before Jesus Christ ascended into Heaven, among His last words to that early church were, "As my Father hath sent me, even so send I you." Jesus passed down to us the ministry of reconciliation.

God has given to us an understanding in His Word of the priority of the ministry, getting the Word of God from one human being to another through the power of the Holy Spirit of God.

While visiting the mission control center of NASA, near Houston, I happened to see their mission statement on the wall of the room where they track all the space shuttle activities. Their mission statement read, "To always be aware that suddenly and unrepentantly, we may find ourselves in a role where our performance has ultimate consequences." I'll never forget reading that. In other words, there are some things that happen in our lives that we will never be able to change later.

"Suddenly and unrepentantly, we may find ourselves in a role where our performance has ultimate consequences."

You may find yourself in that role tomorrow. God may bring you across the path of someone and open that door where you might make the difference in someone's life. First Peter 3:15 states: "But sanctify the Lord God in your hearts: and be ready always to give an answer to every man that asketh you a reason of the hope that is in you with meekness and fear." Be ready at your job place to reach out and teach someone about the Saviour. The calling on my life is getting out the Word of God—not doing a job. It is the priority of the Christian life to be a witness for Jesus Christ.

# The Privilege of the Ministry

It is a great privilege not only to be a Christian but also to be involved in telling someone else about Jesus Christ. I have had some opportunities in my life to meet some interesting people, but nothing has ever given me joy in life like leading someone else to Jesus Christ. Nothing matches it. It is a sorrow to me if I go a period of time and do not see someone saved. If you have never led someone to Christ, I want to challenge you to pray for God to use you in the ministry.

## God Has Given Us a Specific Ministry

The privilege of the ministry is found in the fact God has given to all of us a specific ministry. If you were to receive a personal call from the President of the United States asking you to carry a letter to someone and give it to that person, would you think nothing of it? Most likely you would be surprised and honored to be asked to do something for the President. Yet how much more does it mean to you that the King of Kings and Lord of Lords has given you a specific ministry in sharing the Word of God!

> *It is our great privilege to serve as an ambassador for Jesus Christ.*

## God Has Given Us a Specific Office

Not only has God given us a specific ministry, but He has also given each of us a privileged office. You may not be a pastor or teacher, but II Corinthians 5:20 tells us what we all are in Christ: "Now then we are ambassadors for Christ, as though God did beseech you by us: we pray you in Christ's stead, be ye reconciled to God." We can really begin to sense the awesome privilege of being involved in the ministry. An ambassador is a person sent from one country to another for the purpose of

142

representing the affairs of the sovereign power that deputized him. It is our great privilege to serve as an ambassador for Jesus Christ. We are not to run around pointing out only the errors of the world, but our primary responsibility is to publish the good news that God has given us in His Word. What a joy it is to serve!

In the last few years our ministry has grown, and the responsibilities have become heavier. Although there is much more administration, I do not ever want to forget what ministry really is. Ministry is not administration or working with engineers, building programs, or getting a really organized filing cabinet. It is going out with the Bible, finding a real, live person, and telling him the good news of salvation. I hope you realize there is a calling on your life to be involved as an ambassador of Jesus Christ.

Adoniram Judson was a great Baptist missionary who ministered in Burma for eighteen years without ever taking a furlough. In fact, he was in Burma for six years before he ever had his first convert. By some people's standards, Adoniram Judson was a terrible failure because he didn't have five thousand saved in his first year. But, thank God, the requirement of ministry is faithfulness and not a particular number.

Burma was a hard place for Adoniram Judson. He went through many difficulties and trials, which included having to take his wife, put her on a ship, and watch her leave the harbor for England. His heart began to break, and he wrote in his diary, "If only somehow we could have found some quiet resting place here on this earth where we could have spent the rest of our days here in peace away from these burdens." His diary continued to say, "But life is short, and millions of Burmese are perishing, and I am the only person on this earth who has attained their language in order to communicate the truth of the Bible. I must tell them the good news."

Adoniram Judson understood that he was an ambassador for Jesus Christ. Some of you may be the only ambassador for Jesus Christ where you work. You are God's representative there.

# The Power of Ministry

Sometimes we may not have all the physical power we would like to have. Sometimes we may get weary, but that is when we can thank God that the power is not of us. The Bible says in II Corinthians 5:21, "For he hath made him to be sin for us, who knew no sin; that we might be made the righteousness of God in him."

## The Gospel

The power of the ministry is in the Gospel of Jesus Christ itself. It is not just people with charisma or the gift of teaching that God uses. God wants to use everybody. The power of God is not found in someone's oratorical ability; it is found in the Gospel of Jesus Christ. The power does not have to be our style. We do not want to convert people to

*Everyone is a person of significance.*

ourselves. We want them to know Jesus Christ as their Saviour. The Bible calls us earthen vessels. Although our vessels are made of clay, we have a treasure in us which is Jesus Christ. "I am crucified with Christ: nevertheless I live; yet not I, but Christ liveth in me..." (Galatians 2:20). Everyone is a person of significance.

Jesus Christ became the direct object of our sin and took our sentence. Jesus Christ became sin for us when He hung on that cross. The reason the veil was rent in two and the skies were darkened was that the Father could no longer look upon the Son who bore in His body every sin that would ever be committed in this world.

The Bible elaborates on what happens because Christ took on that sin. Second Corinthians 5:17 says, "Therefore if any man be in Christ, he is a new creature:

145

old things are passed away; behold, all things are become new." Romans 1:16 says, "For I am not ashamed of the gospel of Christ: for it is the power of God unto salvation to every one that believeth; to the Jew first, and also to the Greek." Even the most feeble-speaking or shy person who ventures out to give a tract with the Gospel can be used, filled, and blessed by God.

I will never forget the first time I was able to see a man and woman come to get saved. I was nineteen years old and preaching in a little church near Indio, California. One Sunday I preached from John 3 about being born again. There were seventy people there that particular day.

As I was leading in the invitation song, a couple stepped out and came forward. I asked them why they had come forward, and they told me, "You talked about being born again and knowing for sure you're going to Heaven. We'd like to do that."

I said, "You would?" I forgot all about what I had been doing, and I left the people singing while I took the couple into a back room and shared the Gospel. It was then that Fred and Alice Riley received Christ as Saviour.

About a year before Fred passed away, he wrote me a letter that told me how much he loved me and thanked me for preaching that gospel message nearly twenty years before. I keep that letter to this day, because the most significant things in my life revolve around people's getting saved. Fred and Alice didn't get saved because I was a great preacher. They got saved because the Gospel is the power of the ministry.

### The Holy Spirit

Second, the power of the ministry is the Holy Spirit of God. Acts 1:8 says, "But ye shall receive power, after that the Holy Ghost is come upon you: and ye shall be witnesses unto me both in Jerusalem, and in all Judæa, and in Samaria, and unto the uttermost part of the earth." When we are saved, we are born of the Spirit. The Spirit of God indwells us at that moment. He is constantly working in the hearts of Christians by convicting us, leading us, and showing us. "And they were all filled with the Holy Ghost, and they spake the word of God with boldness" (Acts 4:31). Anything done in our own strength is bound to fail miserably. We want victory to come by God's strength.

# Conclusion

Are you in the ministry? Are you engaging someone with the eternal truths of the Scriptures? The Bible says in

II Corinthians 5:18, "And all things are of God, who hath reconciled us to himself by Jesus Christ, and hath given to us the ministry of reconciliation." God has put into your hands a responsibility. What are you going to do with it? "As my Father hath sent me, even so send I you."

> *The power of the ministry is the Gospel itself accompanied by the Spirit of God in our lives.*

In II Timothy 2:2 Paul writes to Timothy, "And the things that thou hast heard of me among many witnesses, the same commit thou to faithful men, who shall be able to teach others also." Allow your ministry to influence someone else.

It is not just preachers who can influence. Whom are you bringing along? Christianity is only one generation away from extinction. All it takes is one generation of Christians to get more excited about temporal things than about the real ministry, which is the Word of reconciliation. Service is important, but prioritize the ministry of reconciliation that God has given you.

The priority of the ministry is transferring the Word. The privilege of the ministry is that sinners like us receive an ambassadorship to represent the King of Kings and the Lord of Lords. The power of the ministry is the Gospel itself accompanied by the Spirit of God in our lives.

As I stood in NASA's control room, part of the mission statement impacted me: "to recognize that the greatest error is not to have tried and failed, but that in trying, we did not give it our best effort."

This same goal should be applied to ministry today. Our focus should not be on the numbers of people attending our church. Our focus should be on putting forth our best effort; as the song says, "I wonder, have I done my best for Jesus, when He has done so much for me?" We need to give Jesus our best. It is not merely a matter of trying and failing; it is a matter of giving it our best. The right path for every Christian is the path of biblical ministry.

# Setting the Course

1. For the Christian, life is much more than a career choice. Why?

   _____

   _____

   _____

2. What were the two biblical imperatives that gripped Paul's life and reminded him what the Christian life was all about?

   _____

   _____

   _____

3. Do you remember the day you were saved? Do you still have the *joy of your salvation?*

   _____

   _____

   _____

4. As Christians, what is our purpose for being saved?

_____

_____

_____

5. What is really meant by the word "ministry"?

_____

_____

_____

6. Define true discipleship.

_____

_____

_____

7. What is the theme of the Bible as mentioned in II Corinthians 5:19?

_____

_____

_____

8. According to I Peter 3:15, the Christian should live his life having the expectancy of being able to do what?

 

9. Not only did you receive a specific ministry when you accepted Christ as your Saviour, but you were given a specific office as well. What is it?

 

10. Write out II Corinthians 5:20.

 

11. What is an ambassador? How is the Christian an ambassador?

 

12. What great Baptist missionary labored for over eighteen years in the midst of many trials because he took the office of being an ambassador for Christ so seriously?

_____

_____

_____

13. Where is the power of God found?

_____

_____

_____

14. How long has it been since you were truly involved in God's ministry? Determine to take part today.

_____

_____

_____

## CHAPTER SEVEN

# The Right Leadership

### Becoming Leaders to a New Generation of Christians

*"Now after the death of Moses the servant of the LORD it came to pass, that the LORD spake unto Joshua the son of Nun, Moses' minister, saying, Moses my servant is dead; now therefore arise, go over this Jordan, thou, and all this people, unto the land which I do give to them, even to the children of Israel."*

Joshua 1:1,2

When I accepted Christ as my Saviour in 1972, my Sunday school teacher gave me a Bible. She wrote a couple of inscriptions in it and presented it to me on the occasion of my baptism. As I brought that Bible to church, I would hand it to the guest preachers and ask them to sign the flyleaf. I enjoyed running home and reading the verses they had written down, while considering how those verses may have been a blessing to them. As I grew up in church, collecting preachers' signatures became a hobby of mine.

Not long ago, I was sitting in my study spending some time in meditation, thinking about the upcoming week and some of the things we needed to get done. As I looked up on the shelf, I saw the red-letter gift Bible that had been given to me when I was saved in 1972. I pulled it off the shelf and began to look at it.

I flipped to the back to look at some of the signatures in that Bible. I saw the names of Dr. John R. Rice, Dr. B. R. Lakin, Dr. G. B. Vick, Dr. Jack Hyles, Dr. Monroe Parker, Dr. B. Myron Cedarholm, and many others. Looking at those names brought to my memory a heritage of strong Bible preaching.

I thank God for those who have gone on before, faithfully proclaiming the truth of the Word of God. Yet, in reality, times have truly changed. Most of those wonderful men are now with the Lord in Heaven. Others who once had godly influence are no longer remaining true to the fundamentals of the Faith. Some have fallen prey to different types of sin and temptation. It has become evident to me that Bible-based fundamental ministry is at a crossroads that will require a new generation of leaders to take a stand.

In Joshua, chapter one, Israel is at a similar crossroads. Moses, the servant of the Lord, has died. He has passed off the scene. By observing the children of Israel, certain questions may arise concerning Israel's spiritual decisions. Which way will they go now that Moses is gone? What direction will they take? Will they go back to the golden calf and the idolatry of Egypt, or will they be true to the Word of God and the promises that had been given to them?

In our generation, similar questions may be asked of those who look at fundamental churches. Which way will they go? What direction will they take? Church growth experts will tell us that in order to grow again we must bring in new methods of entertainment and rock 'n' roll music. There are many "golden calves" being brought into the modern-day church. Some churches have sadly followed this advice and are doing whatever it takes to attract a crowd.

In Joshua's day, God wanted His people to claim His promises by going into the Promised Land, and He had devised a specific method for that. God's method is seen in verse 1: "Now after the death of Moses the servant of the LORD it came to pass, that the LORD spake unto Joshua the son of Nun, Moses' minister."

God's method has always been the same. He chooses men and women and calls them to His service, so they might lead the people of God in their generation into the promises of God. May we remember Psalm 75:6: "For promotion cometh neither from the east, nor from the west, nor from the south."

I believe it is God's desire to raise up many men and women who will do their part in taking a stand for the fundamentals of the Faith. I believe He wants people in churches around the world to do their part in their towns for their generation by claiming God's promises.

# Joshua's Résumé

The same God who blessed great men and women of the past wants to bless our lives today. What kind of a man does God choose? What kind of a church will God use? For what kind of people is God looking to lead His people into a blessed future?

### Joshua—a Proven Man

In the life of Joshua, several things can be noted. According to the Scriptures, he was a proven man. He was one of the very few born in Egypt who had made the entire journey with Moses. He was also proven in battle.

*Trials are a part of God's sovereign preparation, that He might use us.*

The Bible says in Exodus 17:8 that there was a tremendous challenge to the children of Israel after the water had come from the

160

rock at Horeb. Remember the saying, "Then came Amalek"? The Amalekites, a picture of the flesh, had come to fight against God's people. The Bible says that when the battle began, Joshua was called upon to lead the Israelites. He "discomfited Amalek and his people with the edge of the sword."

A faith that is not worth testing is a faith that is not worth trusting. God tested Joshua throughout the journey because He intended to use him in a great way in the future. Trials and difficulties are often a part of God's sovereign preparation for our lives so that He might use us in the days ahead.

## Joshua—a Servant

Joshua was also a servant. A look at Joshua's life makes it evident that he was a man who faithfully served and ministered to Moses. In Exodus 24:13 the Bible says, "And Moses rose up, and his minister Joshua." Joshua was referred to as a minister, or a servant.

We are reminded of the Lord Jesus Christ in Mark 10:45: "For even the Son of man came not to be ministered unto, but to minister, and to give his life a ransom for many." Just as Joshua was a servant, so we must recognize the necessity of having a servant's heart toward both the lost and one another. We need to learn that

Jesus Christ repudiates status seeking. "Let this mind be in you, which was also in Christ Jesus: Who, being in the form of God, thought it not robbery to be equal with God: But made himself of no reputation, and took upon him the form of a servant, and was made in the likeness of men: And being found in fashion as a man, he humbled himself, and became obedient unto death, even the death of the cross" (Philippians 2:5–8).

> *Jesus Christ repudiates status seeking.*

When we search the Scriptures to see what kind of a person God uses, we will always find a person with a servant's heart—a Christlike spirit. It is not how many people serve a man but how many people he serves that determines greatness in Christ's service.

## Joshua—a Patient Man

Joshua was chosen because he was also a patient man. He had learned how to wait on the Lord and on the man of God. Joshua learned that the harder the course was, the more rewarding the triumph. Joshua remained faithful throughout the course of his life. In Exodus 24:18 the Bible says, "And Moses went into the midst of the cloud, and gat him up into the mount: and Moses was in the mount forty days and forty nights."

The Bible says in Exodus 32:15 that while Moses was meeting with God and receiving the commandments, Moses turned and went down. Joshua was waiting for him and heard the noise in the camp. While Moses was communing with God, Joshua was somewhere at the foot of the mountain waiting patiently for the man of God—forty days and forty nights of waiting.

I do not know about you, but sometimes I struggle with patience. When I want something, I want it right now. That is probably a true reflection of our culture at large. We want instant coffee, instant copies, instant marriage, instant divorce. We live in an instant day. In God's economy, not everything is instant.

Several years ago we were getting ready for our family vacation. I told my wife to make sure everything was packed and ready. My plan was to leave by 4:00 A.M. so we could reach Barstow by 6:00 A.M. and Flagstaff by 2:00 P.M., in order to miss the desert heat.

My sweet wife began to pack and get things ready. I preached Sunday morning and Sunday night. We went home and got into bed about midnight. We were all ready to leave for vacation that next morning at 4:00

A.M. as I had instructed the family.

There was only one problem—we did not wake up until 8:00 A.M.! We rushed everybody to the car, some still in pajamas. I threw some bags into the car, and we hit the road, somewhat frazzled!

After a while, I asked, "Where are my sunglasses?"

My wife said, "They are in the blue bag."

I called to the back seat and said, "Danielle, could you get the blue bag for me? I need my sunglasses."

After a few minutes she said, "Dad, there is no blue bag."

I calmly said to my wife, "Sweetheart, what blue bag are you talking about?"

She said, "The one that was at the top of the stairs that I told you to get as you were locking the house."

"Oh, that one…"

If you are ever out West, it may be helpful to know that there is a Wal-Mart in Flagstaff, Arizona. We spent a good amount of money there that first night of our vacation—for one reason: we struggled with patience.

Oftentimes there is waste in the work of God and in our spiritual lives because we do not wait on the Lord. We fail to be patient as Joshua was. We fail to remember that our present choices many times will determine our permanent outcome. When we fail to wait on the Lord, we will make mistakes every time.

*It is not how many people serve a man but how many people he serves that determines greatness in Christ's service.*

Psalm 27:14 simply says it this way: "Wait on the LORD: be of good courage, and he shall strengthen thine heart: wait, I say, on the LORD."

Joshua was chosen of God because he had proven himself to be a warrior, he had learned how to serve, and he had learned to wait on the Lord.

## Joshua—a Man of Vision

Joshua was also a man who had a vision that God could use him. In Numbers 13, the spies went into the Promised Land. Ten came back and said there was no way they could conquer the land. Yet the Word of God is very clear that Joshua said in Numbers 14:8, "If the LORD delight in us, then he will bring us into this land, and give it us; a land which floweth with milk and honey."

I have often heard pastors say that their community is the hardest place in the country to build a church. The fact is, there are a lot of "hard places." In some places there are too many Baptists. Other places have too many Catholics or cults. Friend, God is looking past the labels and simply seeing souls that need to be saved. Where is our vision? Joshua had a God-given vision of "the bigger they are, the harder they fall."

> *Our present choices will determine our permanent outcome.*

Twelve people asked us to come to Lancaster in 1986. They could not offer us a salary, health insurance, or even help with the move. On top of that, the church was involved in a lawsuit, the building was for sale, a water main was about to break, and there were debt problems. In spite of all the troubles, there was an overriding truth: God called us. So, we went.

After our move to Lancaster, one of the first things I

did was go to a printer. I had designed a little gospel tract with a picture on it and some different things about the church. I told the printer that I could not pay the previous bill nor the cost of the printing of five thousand tracts, but I promised that I would return in thirty days to pay off the entire bill.

He went ahead and printed those tracts for us, and we began to go knocking on doors. We knocked on about five hundred doors a week for fifty-two straight weeks—telling people about the Lord, winning people to Christ, and bringing them into the house of God.

A few months into that process, I went to a preachers' meeting. I was pretty excited about our new tracts, so I handed them out to all the preachers I met. After a while, I noticed that there were three or four preachers standing in a corner with my tracts in their hands. They were laughing as they looked at the tracts.

I thought, "What's wrong with our tract? Is it my picture? Is a word misspelled?"

I walked up and asked, "Why are you guys laughing at the tract?"

They said, "Brother Chappell, have you read this tract?"

I replied, "Have I *read* it? I *wrote* it."

They said, "We are laughing at what you put in here about an exciting Sunday school program. You do not even have a Sunday school program. How can you say you have an exciting Sunday school program?"

I said, "My wife teaches the nursery through the sixth grade, and she is excited about it. That qualifies us for an exciting Sunday school program."

They said, "Well, we don't know about that, but what is this in the brochure about vibrant music? You do not have a piano player. You are the song leader, and you do not have a choir. How can you say you have vibrant music?"

I said, "I lead the congregational singing, and I am vibrant when I do it. That qualifies us for vibrant music."

They said, "Well, how about this active youth ministry? You do not have a youth pastor. You do not have youth classes. You have never been to a youth camp. How can you put in this brochure that you have an active youth department?"

I said, "You are wrong again. We had a youth activity last Friday night with three teenagers, and one was hyperactive. That qualifies us for an 'active' youth department."

They laughed again, thinking it was funny. I wish those same pastors could visit us now to see how God has blessed. Now there is a vibrant music ministry with a 200-voice choir and a 40-piece orchestra that bring praise to the Lord Jesus Christ every week. Now there is a youth department with 400 to 500 teenagers that are being taught the Word of God. Now there is an exciting Sunday school department with Sunday school teachers teaching the Word of God.

Friend, God can do anything but fail! "Now faith is the substance of things hoped for, the evidence of things not seen" (Hebrews 11:1). God blesses vision and faith, and Joshua was a man *God blesses vision and faith.* mightily used of God because he had faith to believe in God's promise!

Pick up some of the promises of God and claim them as your own. What kind of a person can God use? It has nothing to do with age or social status, but it has everything to do with our faith in Him.

# Joshua's Responsibilities

What exactly did God ask Joshua to do? "Moses my servant is dead; now therefore arise, go over this Jordan, thou, and all this people, unto the land which I do give to them, even to the children of Israel" (Joshua 1:2).

## Lead the People Over Jordan

Joshua's responsibility was to lead the people over Jordan. He was to lead them unto the conquest. The Bible says in verse 11 that Joshua began to challenge the people to "possess the land." His responsibility was to lead the next generation into claiming the promises of God. He was called to be a spiritual leader—a servant leader. There were seven nations of Canaanites to be defeated. There were people who would complain and become discouraged. Someone was needed to give them encouragement.

There would be the lonely times, as in the night Joshua stood and waited outside the city walls of Jericho. There he met the Captain of the Lord of Hosts. Joshua recognized that he was under the authority of Jesus Christ and God was going to give the victory. Joshua realized that God had called him to lead others into the work of God. What a joy it is to be able to serve God in a position of leadership, but how great a responsibility to know that one day we will give to the Lord Jesus Christ an account of our leadership!

## Claim the Land

Joshua was called to lead the people, but it was not just a matter of leadership. He was also called to lead them into claiming the Promised Land and the blessings of God. His leadership was given by God to fulfill the carrying out of God's promises in possessing the land.

Notice what it says in verse 4: "From the wilderness and this Lebanon even unto the great river, the river Euphrates, all the land of the Hittites, and unto the great sea toward the going down of the sun, shall be your coast." This area totals about three hundred thousand square miles of Promised Land.

The sad part is that Israel never claimed more than about ten percent of the Promised Land. The same is true of the average fundamental Christian today. Often we do not claim as many promises as God wants us to claim. Have you claimed your neighbor, your block, your city, your workplace for Christ?

When God gave me the first opportunity to begin pastoring, I was eighteen years old. The vice president of our college told me of a small group of ladies who wanted someone to preach to them on Sunday morning, with the goal of eventually starting a church in that area.

A group of college students including my future wife and me went to this town that first Sunday morning, where I was able to preach my very first message. It was about how God remembered Noah, and it lasted exactly *eight minutes*. In fact, it has become my wife's all-time favorite message. She often asks me to preach that message again. As I preached that morning, something happened in my heart. After the service, the ladies asked if I would come back.

I happily accepted their invitation. The next week we had seven people in attendance, and the week following there were several more. After just a few months, God allowed us to organize a church in this small community. We established a doctrinal statement, and I commuted every Sunday to preach. This church is still going today, supporting about twenty missionaries around the world.

Starting that church was an exciting opportunity. After Terrie and I were married, every Saturday we would go out knocking on doors. One day we knocked on the door of the Houston family. Mrs. Houston answered and informed me that her husband was in the backyard. We found him pulling up onions out of his garden, and believe it or not, he was eating the onions as soon as he plucked them from the ground.

As we walked up, he asked me if I wanted an onion. I wanted to talk to him about Christ, so I took an onion and ate the whole thing. (It was about the size of an apple.) I smelled like onions for a week! After I ate the onion, I said, "Sir, I really came by to talk to you about your relationship with God. If you died right now, do you know where you would spend eternity?"

He said, "Well, I guess I really don't know about that."

Among the onions that day, I was able to lead Karl Houston to the Lord. Later his wife and children were saved. Several months later, Karl approached me about helping with the special music. He said he would have Sunday morning's special music ready. He was going to sing "Just a Closer Walk With Thee." I figured you could not go wrong with that, so Karl got together with Barbara, our pianist. Barbara did not really like Karl, but they got together and worked on "Just a Closer Walk With Thee."

When I showed up for church that Sunday morning, there was a big amplifier with a guitar sitting on the platform. When it came time for the special song, Karl stood up and said in his gravelly voice, "I want to dedicate this song to Pastor."

Barbara started playing the piano, and Karl started singing with his foot on the amplifier. He sang for a while, played for a while, and eventually got through the first couple of verses. Just about the time that I was thinking he was almost done, he looked over at Barbara and said, "One more time, Barbara," and started all over again. It wasn't the best quality of music, but we had an exciting service that morning!

You know, there is nothing more exciting than soul-winning! Yes, it takes patience to lead new Christians, but God will give grace and wisdom, as He did in the days of Joshua.

We have mapped out the area in Lancaster so that nearly three times a year any resident will receive a knock on his door from a Lancaster Baptist Church soulwinner. The Bible tells us in Acts 20:20 that we are to go both publicly and from house to house.

In the neighborhood of one of our church members, a group of Jehovah's Witnesses were knocking on doors. One of our teenagers in the neighborhood noticed them and knew they were Jehovah's Witnesses.

He said, "Mom, quick get me some tracts. I am going to cut them off at the pass."

He grabbed some tracts and started knocking on doors, heading toward them. When he got to them, he said, "I am from the Lancaster Baptist Church. You will have to go somewhere else, because we are already on this street."

They got flustered and went to the other side of the street. He did the same thing again on that side of the street. Finally, they got frustrated enough to get in their cars and leave the area. You know what this teenager was doing? He was claiming his neighborhood for Jesus Christ.

Many times I meet people that are amazed that the pastor of a church would take time to come out and invite them to church. I do not want to be telling others to do something that I am not doing.

Recently, I visited a man who had visited our church. His name was Mike. After visiting for a while, I asked him about where he would spend eternity. He said he knew he was saved, and he would spend eternity in Heaven with Jesus Christ. His family seemed shocked, so I asked him on what he based his salvation.

He began to explain about a time a few months before when he had been suffering from depression. After

175

listening to many self-help tapes, he knew there was no difference. At 5:30 every morning, his radio would go off, and it just happened to be stuck on the Christian radio station. Each morning he would quickly turn it off because he did not like the preaching that convicted his heart.

After a while, he began to listen to the sermons from our pulpit little by little. Mike said to me, "One morning you said, 'Some of you ought to put down those self-help books and tapes and trust Jesus Christ as your Saviour!' When you said that on the radio, I knelt down next to my bed, confessed my sin to the Lord, and asked Him to come into my heart and be my Saviour."

After this wonderful testimony, I turned to his wife and asked, "Do you know for sure that you are on your way to Heaven?"

She replied, "I am Presbyterian."

I said, "That is wonderful, ma'am, but do you know for sure you are on your way to Heaven?"

She said, "No."

I asked her if I could show her from the Bible how to be saved, and a few moments later she, along with her son and daughter, were saved.

The wife then turned to me and said, "Excuse me, Pastor; my mother, who just got in from Korea, is upstairs. She really needs to hear this. If I go get her and bring her down, would you tell me this again, because I want to tell her?"

After a few moments of hearing the Gospel translated into Korean, her mom prayed and got saved. The following Sunday they all got baptized. It is a great joy to serve God in leading others to Christ.

*America desperately needs Christians and churches who will claim the land God has promised to them.*

America desperately needs Christians and churches who will be responsible to claim the land God has promised to them.

## Joshua's Resources

Sometimes a Christian hesitates to serve the Lord because he feels he lacks the proper resources. We are tempted to think that God wants to use us but we do not have what others have.

## God's Presence

Notice what the Bible says in Joshua 1:5: "There shall not any man be able to stand before thee all the days of thy life: as I was with Moses, so I will be with thee: I will not fail thee, nor forsake thee." Joshua's first resource was the very presence of God. The Bible says in Numbers 27:18, "And the LORD said unto Moses, Take thee Joshua the son of Nun, a man in whom is the spirit, and lay thine hand upon him."

To Moses, God said, "Now therefore go, and I will be with thy mouth" (Exodus 4:12). To Joshua, God said, "I will be with thee" (Joshua 1:5). To Jeremiah, God said, "And they shall fight against thee, but they shall not prevail against thee: for I am with thee to save thee and to deliver thee, saith the LORD" (Jeremiah 15:20). To Christians, God says, "Go ye therefore, and teach all nations, baptizing them in the name of the Father, and of the Son, and of the Holy Ghost: Teaching them to observe all things whatsoever I have commanded you: and, lo, I am with you alway, even unto the end of the world" (Matthew 28:19, 20).

Many years ago some preachers were discussing whether or not they should have a citywide campaign. The discussion turned to which preacher they should have preach. Finally, one of the older preachers said,

"Well, I think if we have the citywide campaign, we should have D. L. Moody come and do the preaching."

One of the younger preachers, with a tinge of jealousy in his voice, spoke up and said, "Why Moody? Does Moody have a monopoly on the Holy Spirit of God?"

To which the older preacher replied, "No, but the Holy Spirit of God has a monopoly on him."

As you read verse 5, focus on the phrase, "as I was with Moses, so I will be with thee." We have had a great history in our Bible-believing, fundamental churches; and I am thankful that I serve the same God and can be filled with the same Spirit as that of John R. Rice, Monroe Parker, B. R. Lakin, Dr. Curtis Hutson, and others. The Holy Spirit is available now and is indwelling the life of every believer. He is seeking to empower, to control, and to fill us if we would give ourselves to Him. The Word of God is clear: "And be not drunk with wine, wherein is excess; but be filled with the Spirit" (Ephesians 5:18).

Saturday mornings are busy in our household as we get ready to go soulwinning. My wife and I were trying to get ready, but we were a bit late for the 9:30 soulwinning rally.

As we got into the car that morning, I noticed that the

gas light was on and the tank was empty.

A little perturbed, I said, "Sweetheart, your car is out of gas. Why is your car out of gas?"

Her reply was, "Honey, when we got married, you said that if I would take care of the children and the inside of the house, you would take care of the car and the outside of the house." I did not remember that at all.

On the way to the gas station I realized I did not have my wallet, so I said, "Honey, I am going to need some money when we get to the gas station." I failed to tell her I did not have my wallet.

She said, "Paul, I hate to tell you this, but I forgot my purse. It's at home."

I said, "How can you forget your purse? We have to get gas. We are late. Your purse is at home, and now we have to go back to the house to get a wallet and a purse."

Upon arriving at the gas station, I quickly put the gas in the tank but in the process spilled gas all over my pants and shoes. I got back into the car and drove to our soul-winning visit. On the way over, my wife and I had a "discussion" regarding things like bringing her purse and getting gas. Things began to grow tense between us when the Holy Spirit of God began to convict me.

He did not speak audibly; but if it had been audible, it would have sounded something like this: "Okay, you idiot, in a minute you are going to want My power to be a witness. Right now you are so filled up with yourself that I could never fill you."

At that moment, I pulled the car over to the side of the road. We sat there for a while, and I said, "Terrie, I have been a real idiot this morning. I have been grumbling at you about the gasoline and the purse. I have been wrong. Will you forgive me?"

She forgave me and asked for my forgiveness in return. We prayed together and got back on the road.

We visited Dan and Laurenda Winkler that morning. Dan was a graphic artist in North Hollywood. After a few moments of visiting, I asked if they knew that they would go to Heaven when they died.

They both admitted to thinking about this particular question since they had visited the Sunday before. After just a little while, they both prayed and accepted Jesus Christ as Saviour.

Friend, I am convinced that many times we do not have

God's power in witnessing because we have other things on our minds and filling our hearts. The Bible is very clear that as God was with Moses, so He would be with Joshua. As God was with others, He can be with us. I challenge you to seek God's filling and power today as you serve Him!

## God's Preserved Word

The greatest resource we as believers have is the preserved Word of God. Notice Joshua 1:8: "This book of the law shall not depart out of thy mouth; but thou shalt meditate therein day and night, that thou mayest observe to do according to all that is written therein: for then thou shalt make thy way prosperous, and then thou shalt have good success."

You and I have the Word of God that has been kept for the purpose of meditating on it. If we want to know the God of truth, we must saturate ourselves with the truth of God. We must not simply mark our Bibles, but we must let our Bibles mark us. We must meditate in the Word of God.

This verse also says that we should "observe to do." We are not only to meditate in the Word, but we are to obey it. We are to say, "Lord, what would You have me to do?" When we apply the Word of God in our hearts, He will change our lives.

There is power in the Word of God. The Apostle Paul said in Romans 1:16, "For I am not ashamed of the gospel of Christ: for it is the power of God unto salvation to every one that believeth; to the Jew first, and also to the Greek." It is not my power. It is not my program. It is not my ministry. It is not anything of me. It has

*If we want to know the God of truth, we must saturate ourselves with the truth of God.*

everything to do with the wonderful power of the Word of God. If we will seek that power, we too can claim some "Promised Land" for this generation! We can provide the right spiritual leadership that is so needed today.

The right path in leadership is a path that brings others into the promises of God. May we, like Joshua, enter into His promises today!

183

# Setting the Course

1. For the nation of Israel in Joshua 1, their obedience to God's Word depended upon the leadership of whom?

2. What are some of the methods that church growth experts say a church must use in order to grow?

3. In Joshua's day, what determined whether the children of Israel would experience God's blessings?

4. What is God's method for leadership?

5. What is one vital criterion for being a great leader for God as mentioned in Mark 10:45?

6. Write out Philippians 2:5–8.

7. What is the true measure of a person's or a leader's greatness?

8. In today's society of "instants," what is one characteristic that God finds valuable in a leader?

_____

_____

_____

9. In Numbers 13, as the spies were sent to the Promised Land and then returned with their reports, what did Joshua see that the others did not?

_____

_____

_____

10. When God has given a vision, should circumstances or environment be weighed as important before committing to that vision?

_____

_____

_____

11. What can the position of leadership be at times?

_____

_____

_____

12. What could cause a person to hesitate to serve the Lord?

_____

_____

_____

13. What two resources do we have as Christians that enable us to serve the Lord in any capacity in which He chooses to place us?

_____

_____

_____

# West Coast
# Baptist College

## Modeling

Ministry in a dynamic
independent Baptist church

*Dr. Mark Rasmussen directs students
preparing for a day of soulwinning.*

## Mentoring

One life at a time

*Dr. John Goetsch teaches students
in the homiletics class.*

## Motivating

Students by the grace of God and
through the Word of God

(888) 694-9222
4020 E. Lancaster Blvd.
Lancaster, CA 93535
Dr. Paul Chappell, President
Dr. John Goetsch, Exec. Vice President
Dr. Mark Rasmussen, Vice President

*Dr. Paul Chappell challenges hearts
through the preaching of the Word of God.*

# Other titles also available

## To Seek and To Save
*Soulwinning manual and workbook*

A great resource for your church soulwinning ministry, this soulwinning manual has been used to train thousands of soulwinners all over the country. Step-by-step, the reader is instructed in how to communicate the Gospel to a lost person. A companion workbook is also available for class sessions.

## Daily in the Word
*Discipleship manual and materials*

Start your discipleship ministry today with this manual that can be used individually or in an organized discipleship ministry within the church. Teacher's edition, training video pack, and student editions are all available.

## Monthly Leadership CDs

This monthly CD subscription will provide you with a helpful biblical leadership lesson from Dr. Paul Chappell, a companion outline, and a special notebook to hold one year's worth of material. Each month you will receive a compelling, insightful lesson to encourage and equip you for ministry leadership. *Striving Together* is perfect for staff meetings, lay leadership development, or personal growth. Call today to subscribe!

**Sample titles include:**
- Leading in a Hostile Culture
- Structuring Your Ministry to Develop Leaders
- Project Management and Completion
- Development of an Annual Plan
- The Work of the Ministry
- Establishing a Soulwinning Ministry
- Leading through a Building Program

To receive a complete catalog, call
**800.201.7748**, or visit us on our
website at **www.strivingtogether.com**.

Striving Together
P u b l i c a t i o n s

4020 E. Lancaster Blvd. • Lancaster, CA 93535

*For a complete list of books available from the Sword of the Lord, write to Sword of the Lord Publishers, P. O. Box 1099, Murfreesboro, Tennessee 37133.*

*(800) 251-4100*
*(615) 893-6700*
*FAX (615) 848-6943*
*www.swordofthelord.com*

*For a complete list of books available from the Sword of the Lord, write to Sword of the Lord Publishers, P. O. Box 1099, Murfreesboro, Tennessee 37133.*

*(800) 251-4100*
*(615) 893-6700*
*FAX (615) 848-6943*
*www.swordofthelord.com*